# Warning:

## This Manual contains highly sensitive information and is intended solely for use by the employees and management of companies and organizations.

Readers must personally be sure that it never falls into the wrong hands. The enemy is everywhere. The enemy is always listening. The enemy wants our intelligence! The enemy is your customer. Should this book fall into the wrong hands, it can inflict serious damage to the cause to which millions of people have committed themselves fully every day-- chasing away the hordes of jerks who endeavour to keep us from our real work. Since customers' reactions are unpredictable, employ extensive safety measures when possessing a copy of this Manual to be sure they don't pick it up and learn the truth about our mission. In every case, therefore, avoid contact with customers, consumer organizations and sympathetic members of the press, such as Marketplace, Consumer Watch and other reprehensible television programs. Finally, readers would do well to exercise extreme caution when transporting, storing, reading or otherwise using this book. The publisher and author explicitly disclaim all liability for any consequences caused by careless or inappropriate use.

## With that, let us begin with:
## Directives to Prevent the Spurious Use of This Book

Observe all the following directives whenever you read, store or transport this book:

- ✗ Disguise the book with a neutral cover, preferably brown paper. If it suits you, use the jacket of a recent management bestseller or any other cover which would suggest the complete absence of any useful content.

- ✗ Always read this book behind closed doors whenever customers and other strangers of dubious origin are in your field of vision.

- ✗ Be on constant alert for individuals who may try to unobtrusively read over your shoulder.

- ✗ Beware of hidden cameras and security scum who suspect you have privileged knowledge.

- ✗ Never leave this book unattended at your place of employment. Keep it in a locked drawer, cupboard or safe.

- ✗ NEVER, under ANY circumstance, should you take this Manual home with you or bring it to any other hazardous location where others may read it.

- ✗ Never loan this Manual to others, including your partners and colleagues. You could be held liable for any possible damages they may cause by having read your copy.

- ✗ When you have mastered the contents of this Manual, swallow it.

POD edition.

ISBN: 978-1-4392-3511-9
This is a publication of the Customer Chasers Club

# HOW TO CHASE YOUR CUSTOMERS AWAY

## and enjoy work again!

The Ultimate Manual on Taking Action to Frustrate Customer Expectations with Inferior Products, Substandard Services and an Arrogant Attitude

Guido Thys

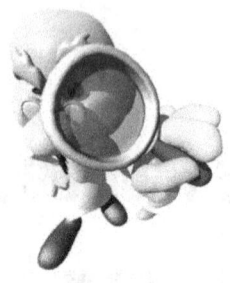

# Table of Contents

# Introduction:
# Why You Need This Book

The International Customer Chasers Club, the largest professional organization in the world, was founded on November 20th, 2002.

Its membership includes the entire working population of the United States (51.600.000), Canada (15.870.000), Australia (8.300.000) and New Zealand (2.000.000), ready to do their own bit for the cause of chasing customers away. The Club's goal is to offer a forum for the exchange of knowledge and experiences in the working world, and thereby help its members increase their enjoyment of their work.

The Club meets one of the biggest latent needs of the world: Worldwide, customers prevent millions of hardworking souls from doing their real work. Any one who is a customer can take a good look around them and see it with their own eyes. Yes, that means you, too.

Here's what I mean:

In most companies, policies, processes and procedures have been developed to drive customers--the jerks and the enemy--as far away as possible, and as quickly as possible.

Here's what I mean: In most Some companies are more successful than others and enormous differences can be found between them.

The Customer Chasers Club wants to do something to remedy this.

If, while reading this Manual, the absurd and improbable event arises that, with complete conviction, you continue in your customer-friendly habits, then stop reading. This is the only answer to the question, "but what if..." Moreover, you will be mercilessly tossed out of the Customer Chasers Club by the Blackball Committee. Rightly so! Insubordination and potential sabotage we don't need.

But you're not customer friendly. Perhaps you were at one time. Even I, the Customer Chasers Club President, have recovered from being that way. With more than 800 presentations and workshops for 90,000-plus participants, I've become one of the world's most requested speakers in the field of customer orientation. My keynote point of view? I've given up! People are driving their customers away en masse. I was mistaken. I am now giving my clients what they want: help and assistance in their daily, impassioned battle against the customer.

This Manual then, is a compilation of the best of customer abuse. My hope is that the strategies, tactics and insults will become both part of your daily work-world guide and your source of inspiration.

## Political Manifesto # 1 :
## Customers are jerks

# Customers are jerks who prevent us from getting our real work done.

As president of the Customer Chasers Club, I've done extensive research, using scientific methods, into the behaviour and attitudes used with customers. Unlike the usual avenues of research,[2] these methods guarantee results that are reliable and true.

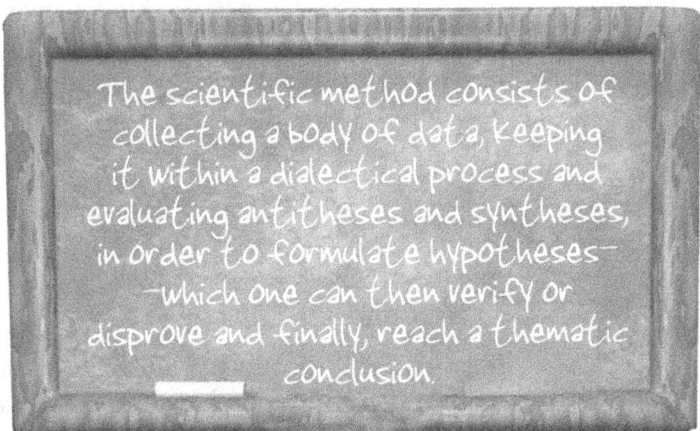

The scientific method consists of collecting a body of data, keeping it within a dialectical process and evaluating antitheses and syntheses, in order to formulate hypotheses— which one can then verify or disprove and finally, reach a thematic conclusion.

This researcher came to the following conclusions through a study which:

✗ covered a combined period of 100 years;

✗ consulted more than 35,000 employees and managers from hundreds of companies and organizations;

✗ these organizations belonged to the three categories (non-profit, for profit, and we'd-like-to-be-for-profit-but-it-ain't-goin'-so-well);

✗ study was performed in various countries where dealing with customers is a way of life.

[1] Readers who know how scientific research works, are already on to what's really going on: the author has talked to two people who each have 50 years experience (probably his parents), and presented his findings to an incoherent audience of misfits behind closed doors in untraceable third world countries, and no one protested loud enough to be heard up front.
[2] In scientific texts there are always lots of footnotes. That's why we thought we'd throw in a few here too.

The objective of the study was to determine what the average employee and manager in the average organization think about the average customer. This study has irrefutably demonstrated that the behaviour of people who come in contact with the enemy (the customer) is determined by a profound and common conviction. The findings became the "Law of Thys," and simultaneously, the vision of the Customer Chasers Club.

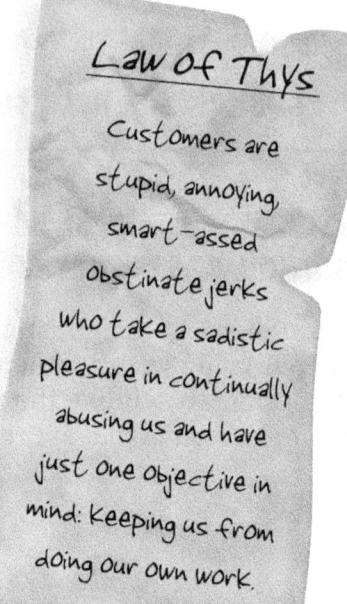

**Law of Thys**

Customers are stupid, annoying, smart-assed obstinate jerks who take a sadistic pleasure in continually abusing us and have just one objective in mind: keeping us from doing our own work.

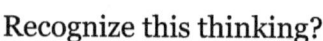

Recognize this thinking?

When reading the Law of Thys, you probably experienced a bittersweet sense of recognition. You felt the urge arise within you to stand up and shout aloud: "Yes! I knew it! Finally someone who understands me!" It's not strange or unusual to experience such a reaction; neither should you suppress this feeling.

It is perfectly normal to allow this outburst of joy to be accompanied by dances of delight, by exchanging high-fives with your colleagues, etc. In the unlikely event that you do not feel this way, do not worry! Do not despair. Years of indoctrination, aided by quality programs, customer-satisfaction campaigns and, more recently, Customer Relationship and experience Management literature have left their mark on all of us and clouded our clearer outlook on reality.

Fortunately, the Division of the Customer Chasers Club you developed a brainwashing program that will deliver you from your illusions permanently. The added bonus is this: the program consists of just three simple steps:

**Question 1:**
Have you, yourself, ever been a customer anywhere?
The answer: Yes (of course).
(You have now completed 1/3 of the brainwashing. You see, it's not so bad after all.)

**Question 2:**
Have you ever gone shopping in a good mood, with money to burn, and come home broke and pissed off? Did you then ask yourself, "what in heaven's name did I do to deserve the abuse accompanying every transaction?"

The answer: Yes (of course).
The explanation: Read the Law of Thys. Customers are a pain. Whenever you walk into a store or contact a company for information or services, the person you deal with is always saying to him/herself, "Oh shit, another jerk, and I was just going to start on my real work. "

**Question 3:**
Do you know that feeling of being interrupted "just when I was going to...?" It's almost as if the jerks are on a stakeout in a building across the street, just lying in wait until you are about to begin something important. They then proceed to impinge upon your time, by phone, by e-mail, or in person and make unreasonable demands. The answer: Yes (of course).

End of maneuver! Now wasn't that easy?

You see that you really do agree with the Law of Thys!

Ok, now you're with us again. Or, in true management lingo: in "strategic and customer alignment" with the rest of the working population of your country.

Or, again, you are if you don't belong to that group of shirking lowlifes, who, in this phase of the learning process exclaim, "Yes, but I don't work directly with our customers, so I'm out of the line of fire!"

Naturally you do not belong to that particular group of readers. However, I'm not taking any chances, so the following paragraph is compulsory reading. Everyone has customers. Whether you like it or not, the enemy is omnipresent. Even if external customers are not jerkering you, inevitably, the reality of internal customers is making your life miserable. A customer is someone with whom you share a barter process: you give something and you get something in return. (It's unfortunate that you always end up with less than when you started, but you already knew that. That's why you're reading this Manual.)

Barter processes are a nightmare for us all. You don't need external customers to have one. Bosses and other management types, colleagues, team mates, "subordinates," departmental staff, advisors: all of them are waiting in line to give you work to do that you really don't need or want, work they could do better themselves. Conclusion: the enemy really is lying in ambush.

So, the next step is: action!

What can we learn from others? In other words, if everyone is convinced that customers are jerks, and those jerks are everywhere, how are they dealt with?

Studies have been done on this as well.

Research shows that, within most organizations, techniques, tactics and strategies have been justifiably developed to defend themselves against the increasing onslaught of gangs of jerks.

Unfortunately, not all are successful in their defense. Some organizations have made fruitless attempts: they reserve budgets, hire in-house consultants, set up training courses, install software, redesign their processes, etc. Conversely, others need only snap their fingers and all the jerks disappear like a snowball in hell. What is their secret?

It's very simple. The recipe for success has just two ingredients:

**1. Clarity:** as in all aspects of business management, it is absolutely crucial to make radical choices when dealing with the enemy. There are no grey areas-- it's either black or white. In a successful organization, your working enjoyment is the common good and absenteeism no longer exists. To whomever you pose the question "What do you do for a living?", the answer, without hesitation and with complete conviction, will invariably be:

# CHASING CUSTOMERS AWAY!

Obviously, employees will express this in other terms. They'll talk about processes, procedures, consultations, self-teaching teams, sounding board groups, systems, protocol, following policy, etc. When looking at it from the customer's viewpoint, however, it all comes down to one thing: chasing the customer away. And it's a damn good thing.

The query "What do you do for a living?" is often a somewhat sensitive question in higher corporate circles and should rather be formulated as "What is your core business?" That is "management-speak" and is understood better. Here too, a loud chorus of "Chasing Customers Away!" is heard, although it sounds no less different here than when spoken above.

Phrases like strategic planning, long-term vision, leadership, management style, joint ventures, sound ventures, balanced scorecard, TQM, benchmarking, shareholder value, empowerment, delegation, helicopter view, innovation and CRM are scattered all around you. But we know that chasing customers away is truly the main objective.

**2. Teamwork**: (Under discussion more fully in the next chapter.)

Studies have shown that most people whistle or hum on their way to work. Then why do they cease whistling and humming when they hit the front door of a place of business? The answer is very simple: because customers are constantly annoying them during their working hours. This is how it should be:

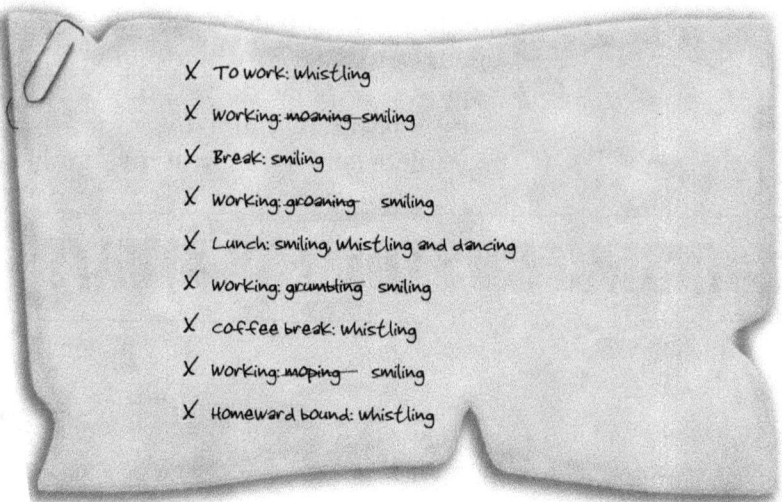

X To work: whistling

X working: ~~moaning~~ smiling

X Break: smiling

X working: ~~groaning~~ smiling

X Lunch: smiling, whistling and dancing

X working: ~~grumbling~~ smiling

X coffee break: whistling

X working: ~~moping~~ smiling

X Homeward bound: whistling

This, however, is the reality:

During coffee breaks (which become increasingly longer, understandably so, as most employees are mere humans) and lunch, there is a little spark of pleasure, but it only really gets better after working hours. That's why everyone whistles on the way home from work.

Self-defense is included in the Human Rights Declaration. Creating and maintaining an enclave of peace and quiet and working enjoyment is an integral part of it. Building a Wall of China around one's own "comfort zone" should be included at the top of each job description. The word "comfort" is not just a play on words, but also a bitter emotional necessity.

The next few pages will depict an analysis of the typical ways in which customers subtly creep up, attack and ruin you. (Not suitable for tender souls.) First, figure out what you really think of customers in this brainstorming exercise on the next page:

## Brainstorm

Fill in a minimum of 12 of the worst names you can think of to call your customers. Hang this little list on the wall, just in case you ever doubt the necessity of chasing the jerks away.

You can do this alone or brainstorm with your colleagues. You have 30 seconds for this drill.

| | |
|---|---|
| **1.** | |
| **2.** | |
| **3.** | |
| **4.** | |
| **5.** | |
| **6.** | |
| **7.** | |
| **8.** | |
| **9.** | |
| **10.** | |
| **11.** | |
| **12.** | |

# The loss of working enjoyment

**1.** You love your job. You hum your way through the day. You have heaps of time for your own work. There is not a cloud in the sky. Life is good.

**2.** Then, unwittingly, you make one small error: a customer spots you and poses an ostensibly simple question. Now there's a blemish on an otherwise successful day. You're done for in no time.

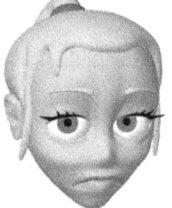 

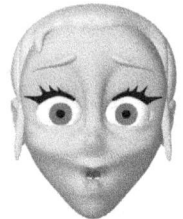  

**7.** Your good mood is disappearing quickly. Fate reveals itself before your very eyes: you're destined to spend the rest of the day catering to this jerk—the best-case scenario.

**8.** Another customer has discovered that you're on the run without cover and has tracked you down. You receive an additional "request." Run for your life!

**9.** Your working environment is turning against you, because your colleagues are sick of you continually coming along with new problems, which, after all, only detract from their working enjoyment.

# through customer contact

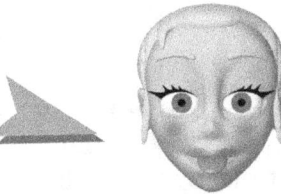

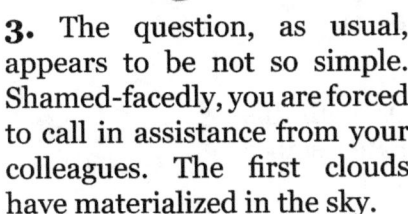

**4.** The day threatens to turn out much differently than you planned. The jerk is causing more work than you presumed. You develop somber suspicions.

**3.** The question, as usual, appears to be not so simple. Shamed-facedly, you are forced to call in assistance from your colleagues. The first clouds have materialized in the sky.

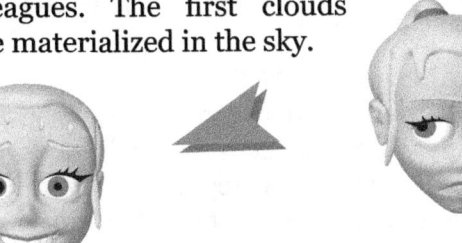

**5.** To make matters even worse, the client insists on a quick response. As if you didn't have enough to do, now you have to spend time on this sort of ridiculous conversation.

**6.** You break into a cold sweat. Your colleagues don't feel like answering the customer any more than you do. You find yourself between a rock and a hard place. You attempt to get rid of the enemy, but fail miserably.

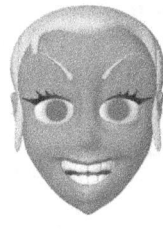

**11.** Your job has become hell. You hardly make it through the day. You never get around to doing your real work. You've become a sitting duck for every jerk around, and the social outcast of the office. One mistake with catastrophic consequences, and it's your own bloody fault.

**10.** You are fast approaching your boiling point. You are obliged to swallow question after question from customers. You're forced to face the painful reality: you can pretty much forget your own personal freedom.

Years ago, the well-known firm of consultants, McKinsey, conducted a study into the ways in which organizations chase away their customers. The results are universal and edifying for all members of the Customer Chasers Club.:

### Death 1%
These are the so-called 'natural causes'. Although very effective, it is not advisable to lend nature a helping hand in this way. The one percent of jerks that disappear in this manner is simply an added bonus.

### Move 3%
Also considered a natural cause, however, with this phenomenon you *can* lend a helping hand. Remember the name of our club, you can take it literally!

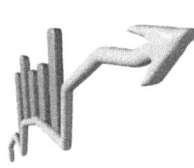

### Other personal contact 5%
This has to do with the customer's tendency to do business with the company where his/her brother-in-law works. Helping the customer in this category is a lengthy and time-consuming activity. You want to try introducing unattached family members of your customers to single family members of employees of the competition? You can better simple serve off your own customers. Just as absurd, but far less time-consuming.

### Price 9%
Even if you are giving your product or service away for free, customers will always want it cheaper. Try tripling your prices and you'll either drive away the enemy in droves or make salesman of the year.

### Dissatisfaction with a product 14%
The fine print, a little fiddling with the product: these are endless sources of working enjoyment. However, there is one important disadvantage: they bring with them a string of complaints from here to Tokyo. And back. So, not really productive, after all.

### Apathy 68%
The most effective technique, then, proves also to be the one with the highest entertainment value. In everything you do for your customer – or better, everything you don't do -, in everything you say to him/her – or don't say –, you are transferring the message: "you're nothing to me!" "Jerk!" "Get lost!"

**Political Manifesto # 2 :**

**Teamwork is essential**

# "An obstructionist who lets the jerks in through the back door is like beating your head ainst a brick wall."

Chasing Customers Away is only possible thanks to a concerted effort by **everyone** in the organization. If your company employs 250 people, for example, there is absolutely no point in having 249 of them chasing customers away at the front door if there is one saboteur who lets them in the back door. This is beating your head against a brick wall, which is known worldwide as the second most absurd activity invented by humankind. The first is customer service. So - Teamwork! All shoulders to the wheel! A united front against the jerks!

Every self-respecting person belongs to at least 5 or 6 teams, the most important advantage being that you spend most of your time in team meetings and *can't* be bothered by the jerks at all.

Putting together a team should be approached with the greatest care possible. A large and diverse team offers at least four advantages.

## Team Advantages

**More colleagues continue being unavailable for the customer**

**The customer must go through more steps and will get lost**

**Your working enjoyment increases through good company**

**You can take a day off without the enemy gaining any ground**

Compose these teams of as many specialists as possible, and other wise owls, who swoop down from as many different disciplines possible, and who know as little as possible about the business. Use the table on the next page to do an inventory.

## Brainstorm

Invent a concrete request by a customer. Write down below which colleagues, suppliers or advisors cannot fulfill or respond to this request. Include how you can involve them. You can complete this exercise alone or in a brainstorming session with your colleagues. You have three minutes for this task. Looking ahead to the following pages is not sporting.

| | Customer request: |
|---|---|
| 1. | |
| 2. | |
| 3. | |
| 4. | |
| 5. | |
| 6. | |
| 7. | |
| 8. | |
| 9. | |
| 10. | |

Following are a few suggestions for the types of team members who work well together (read - who can thoroughly screw things up for the customer):

## Specialists

Teamwork can be very effective especially with those specialists who cannot contribute anything useful to actually realizing the customer's wishes. Their most important contribution always consists of making an assignment or order infinitely more complex, so that it eventually becomes impossible to fulfill.

## Natural talent

Those who have a natural talent in devising customer-hostile techniques can always find a way to impede the smooth progress of a transaction, and to make the customer feel like there are more important things on this earth than meeting their endless series of wishes and whims.

## Middle Management

Furthermore, the efforts of a wide spectrum of middle management types who meddle with operations behind the scenes are essential. In this way, these walking debit items can safeguard the work in progress. The work must not only meet various quality requirements and safety and environmental regulations, moreover, it must also substantially

surpass the specified minimum figures. Or, they can also assess each minute detail on its *strategic alignment*.[*]

## Management

Finally, it is up to the management to directly or indirectly make it impossible for you to fulfill customer wishes. This can be done directly by giving practical advice with regard to carrying out the job; the management generally has so little experience with this that the loss of time is only increased. Indirectly, the management can withhold indispensable materials and equipment from the teams. Periodic, mindless cost-saving rounds are the most radical method for this.

---

(*) Having parts of an organization or concrete activities in "strategic alignment", simply means that they fit within every vision, strategy, ethical guideline and procedure which all supervisors, directors, managers and leaders have agreed upon – after decennia of discussion. In short, they have not the slightest practical purpose anymore.

## External consultants

Contributions from outside enrich an organization. That is, the contribution to decision making and implementation produces extra material for discussion, and the customer is once again kept from achieving his/her goal.

## Customers

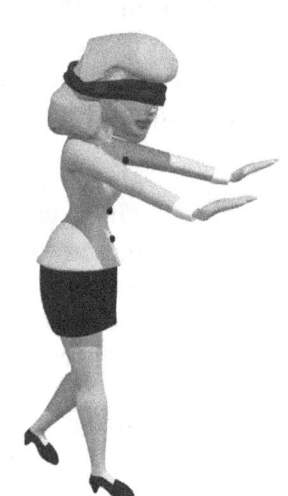

Involvingthecustomer him/herself in the activities preceding a delivery produces a particularly good entertainment value. Under the guise of advisory bodies, sounding board groups and customer satisfaction surveys, you create the impression that the wishes of the customer are actually beingtaken into account. The subtle humor exists in the fact that this could be no further from the truth, and that you actually use the customer's input solely to prolong the internal processes ad infinitum.

This subtle combination of elements can reach uncommon heights if there is sufficient enthusiasm behind it. Moreover, computerization can be dragged in, in order to cast everything into an ironclad process that can never again be altered. The ERP (Enterprise Resource Planning) and CRM (Customer Relationship Management) software have in the recent past proven worldwide to have an absolutely devastating influence on customer orientation.

To the right, a simple depiction of the settlement of an insurance claim by a well-organized insurance company is given.

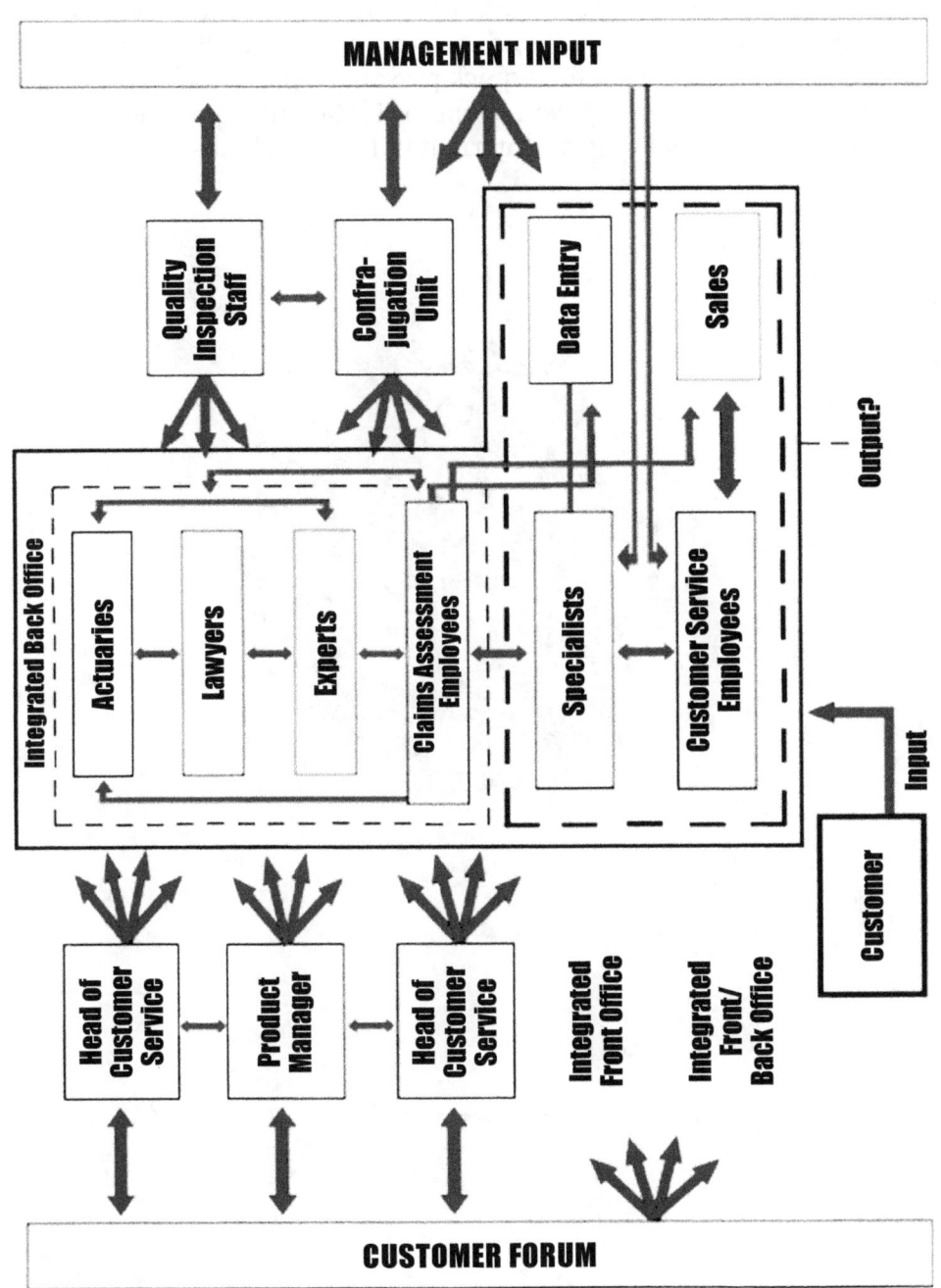

You can form ad hoc teams at any time and close them down again just as quickly. If your colleague Hank is talking with a customer, you can drive the latter definitively around the bend by continually phoning this colleague, by dropping by for a quick personal discussion, by making a deafening racket in an adjacent room, or by talking with others at the top of your voice about the moron right in front of Hank.

## The Chasing Customers Away Attitude Test

If all is well, then you should be ready to wage war against the enemy and drive the jerks from your 'milieu' for good. That just leaves the technique. Afore we can embark on that, you must pass the next test.

With the assistance of this handbook you can chart out your own attitude and motivation. Circle the option which best describes your emotions. Count up your score and look in the Analysis to see how your mental resistance is holding up (or sagging). Use your answers to discover where improvement is necessary. Be honest in your answers. Making a fool of your customers is OK, but painting yourself in a more flattering light will get you nowhere.

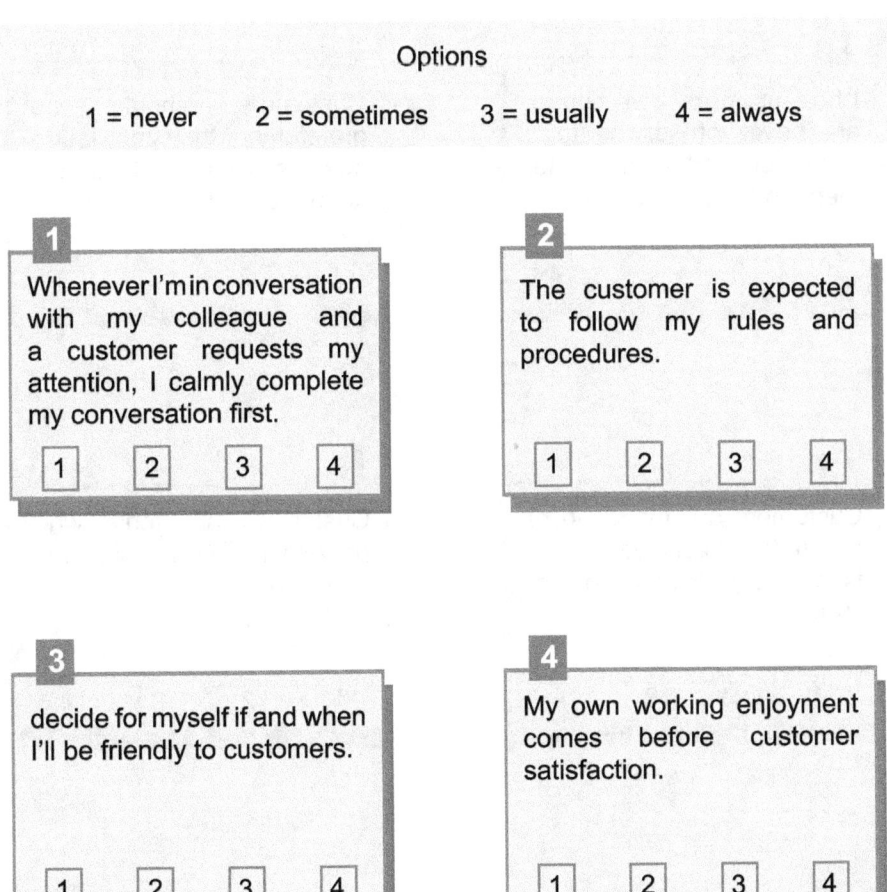

Options

1 = never    2 = sometimes    3 = usually    4 = always

**1**
Whenever I'm in conversation with my colleague and a customer requests my attention, I calmly complete my conversation first.

1    2    3    4

**2**
The customer is expected to follow my rules and procedures.

1    2    3    4

**3**
decide for myself if and when I'll be friendly to customers.

1    2    3    4

**4**
My own working enjoyment comes before customer satisfaction.

1    2    3    4

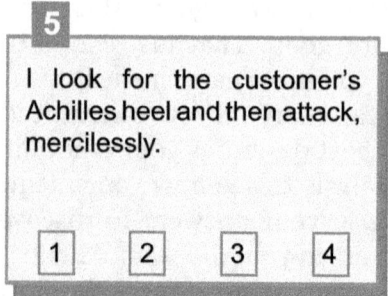

**5**

I look for the customer's Achilles heel and then attack, mercilessly.

| 1 | 2 | 3 | 4 |

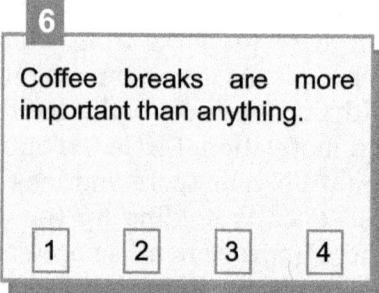

**6**

Coffee breaks are more important than anything.

| 1 | 2 | 3 | 4 |

**7**

I hole up in my own corner, am never of service to a customer, and always refer them on to my colleague.

| 1 | 2 | 3 | 4 |

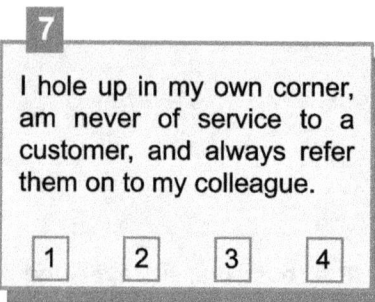

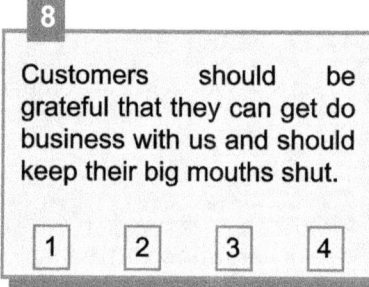

**8**

Customers should be grateful that they can get do business with us and should keep their big mouths shut.

| 1 | 2 | 3 | 4 |

**9**

Customers are made up of psychotic expectations. It is my duty to fight against them.

| 1 | 2 | 3 | 4 |

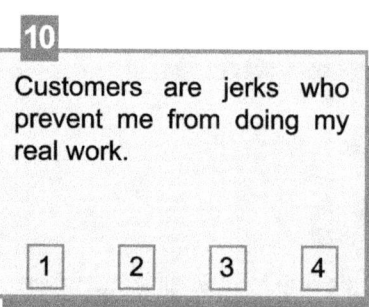

**10**

Customers are jerks who prevent me from doing my real work.

| 1 | 2 | 3 | 4 |

## Analysis

Count up your score and compare them to the categories here below. Don't forget that there is always room for improvement, no matter which level you have achieved.

**40-31**: Super! You are eligible for an Honorary Membership in the Customer Chasers Club. You can apply for your certificate at www.customerchasersclub.nl.

**30-21**: Reasonable, but not nearly good enough. Find some of your colleagues who have scored better and learn from them. Herd a few customers into a closed room and experiment.

**20-10**: Rotten! There is absolutely no point in your reading the following chapters, since your understanding of morals and values is completely distorted. Reread the preceding chapters, get some therapy and try again.

# The three fronts: Customer expectations

## "Customer needs? A good offense is the best defense!"

A good strategist knows the battlefield. He knows where he can take his advantage; he knows the enemy's weak spots. He can predict the ambushes, foresee the enemy's next step and can call in his allies.

Customers are an enemy to be feared. They areunderhanded and sly: they pretend to be interested in your products and services, but in fact, they cunningly exact much more from you. A good defense is only possible if you know your enemy. Now would be a good time for a little customer psychology.

If you are not on your guard, you will unsuspectingly fall into one of the hundreds of traps the enemy has set for you. The moment you think the transaction has successfully been completed, and/or you have successfully avoided any imaginable (extra) work, the jerk is just stepping up to the starting blocks. He/she's ready to bombard you withendless lists of demands and expectations.

The stress this creates is the foremost, if not the only, cause of work-related ailments and illnesses. Particularly, employees in front-office positions (sales, service, maintenance) are most often in the line of fire. Stress, high blood-pressure, cardio-vascular disorders, alcohol and other addictions, paranoia, nail-biting and general emotional collapse are among the classic syndromes.

## Influence of custumor contact on % Disability

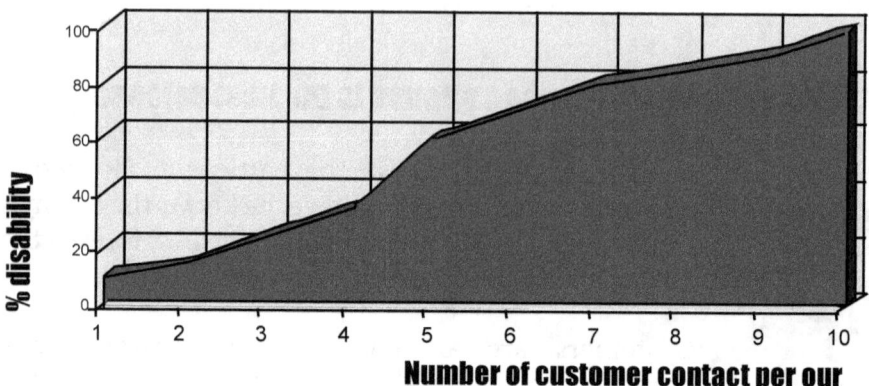

**Customer expectations**

Customers are made up of psychotic expectations. You haven't even finished acceding to the first wish that was hurled at you, before the next one has been launched. The customer is always standing there, looking for a handout Suppliers (of products as well as services) are often blinded by the product or service that the customer purchases from them; they assume that this is the only, or at least the most important, reason why the customer patronizes his business. Unfortunately, the problem is infinitely more complex. You need to be, not doubly, but triply on your guard. Specifically, **three kinds of customer expectations** can be distinguished. All three are constantly present, and each form in their own way a substantial threat to your working pleasure.

On the other hand, they offer the offensive player a hundred thousand chances to wallop the customer 'real good'. The best defense is truly a good offense.

The optimists in our midst will only see this as good news: the more customers want, the more chances there are to thwart them.

# The box: With a Little Help from Pandora

That for which the enemy will fork out his/her money forms the core of the barter process between supplier and customer:

- ✗ products;
- ✗ services;
- ✗ information;
- ✗ and/or combinations thereof.

In short, we could talk about "Boxes" that we push the customer's way.

The jerk expects that these Boxes will have a certain value or usefulness, that it will improve his/her quality of life.

The jerk expects that these Boxes will have a certain value or usefulness, that it will improve his/her quality of life.

This already indicates what our most important objective must be: to send a Trojan horse into the enemy camp. The Box should not deliver any of the advantages that the customer is made to anticipate. Moreover, it will only cost the customer more time, money, energy and health; a box of which Pandora could be truly proud.

This is more complex than you would at first imagine. If the exterior of the Box overtly appears to be useless or dangerous, the jerk will have nothing to do with it and will continue to harass the salesperson until he

does get what he wants. A good Box **looks like** it will deliver the anticipated advantages, until the customer has paid for it.

At that moment, it falls apart, or better yet, it becomes life threatening.

The entertainment value for you – the supplier - is enormous.

Extra complications occur in organizations, which throughout years of mismanagement have implemented various extravagances, such as Total Quality Management programs, money-back guarantees, ISO Certificates and customer awareness groups.

The best manner to deal with the supporters of these excesses is to stimulate them to do their work even better, to raise their requirements even higher and to define even more processes for them. The production of the Boxes will become so bogged down or so expensive that customers will quickly defect to the competition.

A worthy alternative is called "diversification": you make an increasing number of similar-looking Boxes, until the customer eventually needs a university degree to make heads or tails of it. A good example of this is tea. Tea used to be just tea - in a bag. Now, an enormous box is dragged out and beforeyou are actually sipping, a quarter of an hour has passed.

Ladies and gentlemen, space is a service we don't provide anymore in the economy class.

Conversely, you can also increasingly reverse various aspects of the Box over the years. There is a technical term for this: elasticity: You continually test the flexibility and strength of your customers' stamina.

After careful scrutiny, we see thousands of ways to sabotage the Box and get a rise out of the jerk. In the 1960's, Philip Kotler introduced the concept of marketing. On the basis of his famous '4 P's' he outlined which variables can be used to influence the relationship between customer and supplier. It proves to be an ideal way to give form to your tactical plan of attack:

**Product**

**Price**  **Place**

**Promotion**

## Brainstorm

Fill out below a minimum of 12 ways in which you can make your customer's life hell using only your products or services. You can do this alone or in a brainstorming session with your colleagues. You have three minutes for this task. Peeking ahead is not sporting.

| | |
|---|---|
| 1. | |
| 2. | |
| 3. | |
| 4. | |
| 5. | |
| 6. | |
| 7. | |
| 8. | |
| 9. | |
| 10. | |
| 11. | |
| 12. | |

Let's put Kotler's four instruments to work.

**Arch-enemy of the Club**

*One of the most important archenemies of the Customer Chasers Club is Philip Kotler. He wrote his Principles of Marketing in 1967, which systematically teaches companies, marketers and salespeople how they should make their customers happy. It is one of the most reprehensible, dangerous and depressing books we know. It has also been placed high on the list of Revoked Literature.*

## 1. The P for Product

It would be going too far to explore extensively the tens of thousands of ways in which you can use the Box to frustrate customer expectations.

### A selection of possibilities to jerker customers with the aid of products :

- ✗ make products so complex that the enemy can't make heads or tails of it;
- ✗ ensure that the enemy must buy several accessory products before he/she can use the product he has just purchased;
- ✗ the product always just 'happens' to be out of stock;
- ✗ the customer comes to your counter with a product and you inform him/her that is has already been sold to someone else;
- ✗ when wrapping the purchase, you exchange the product that the customer has chosen with a different one, or with a defective or spoiled product, or simply, with an empty box.;
- ✗ the product breaks down the day after the guarantee expires;
- ✗ for food products: de maggots and bugs come crawling out of the product just after the customer gets home;
- ✗ you warn the customer of so much impending doom and disaster and refuse all responsibility for all the possible calamities that can result from use of the product that the customer dare not touch it anymore;
- ✗ have the customer sign piles of legal statements (even when buying two pounds of apples, for instance) so that he immediately changes his mind about making the purchase;
- ✗ for catalogue sales: the product, naturally, is much shoddier in reality than it looks in the picture.

## The product is the decisive factor

The customer is often so desperately looking forward to possessing a product that you can pull almost any trick on him. The amount of time you are willing to invest determines whether or not you will want to do this. Sometimes, solid preparation and teamwork with other suppliers will net you a twofold result: you can take the jerk's money and get rid of him at the same time.

### CASE STUDY

The manager of a SME invested in a completely new IT-infrastructure in order to process the information enquiries and purchases of his clients more quickly. He had calculated that the cost of the investment corresponded approximately with two years salary of someone who processed this by hand. The customer gave an extensive briefing to the hard×ware and software suppliers and put a tight timeframe on it. All of the individual parts were delivered promptly according to schedule and the customer paid the majority of the invoice. The inimitable ingenuity of the suppliers then became appar ent: subsequently, not one of the individual parts appeared to work properly. The hardware was slower than the old system and the software was more complex than the development of a space program. Three months after the installation date, the entrepreneur had lost two years salary on junk and still had to process all enquires and orders by hand. He went bankrupt. The suppliers went on holiday.

Services are the same as products in many respects. They are simply not as tangible and thus, you can sabotage them much more before the enemy becomes aware of it.

## Jerkering your customers with the aid of services.

If you are the supplier of services rather than a product, there are just as many possibilities. You simply have the service performed by a colleague who:

- ✗ knows nothing about it;
- ✗ shows up late;
- ✗ makes a mess of everything;
- ✗ snaps at the customer when he/she comments on it;
- ✗ leaves early;
- ✗ and leaves behind a chaos that will plague the customer for years to come.

## Summary
The enemy becomes a customer and remains a customer only when he gets what he wants. So, in simple terms: don't give him what he wants. Period. The more complex form entails stringing him along endlessly only to deny him what he wants in the end. It's time-consuming but amusing.

GROUNDS FOR EXPULSION

YOU SUPPLY
THE CUSTOMER
WITH THE
PRODUCT

## 2. The P for Price

As we have already read in the previous chapter, price is a rather tricky customer-chasers instrument because the competition has the tendency to adjust her prices to meet yours, *et voilá*: your distinguishing chasers-advantage disappears.

However, this does not mean that price is unimportant. Au contraire. The intention behind chasing customers away lies in realizing a turnover, which will allow you to benefit from your working enjoyment without being disturbed every other minute by the jerk. You raise your prices to such an extent that you can realize your desired turnover with just a few customers per year.

An example in figures:

| | |
|---|---|
| Yearly amount that you need to get by: | € 72.000 |
| Number of customers you can stand: | 12 |
| Margin you must realize per transaction: | € 6.000 |

A piece of cake if you're selling cars, this is a bit trickier if you're selling feathered chickens. In that case, however, you are better armed. Each occupation has its own advantages.

In calculating your prices, you should take the following elements into consideration:

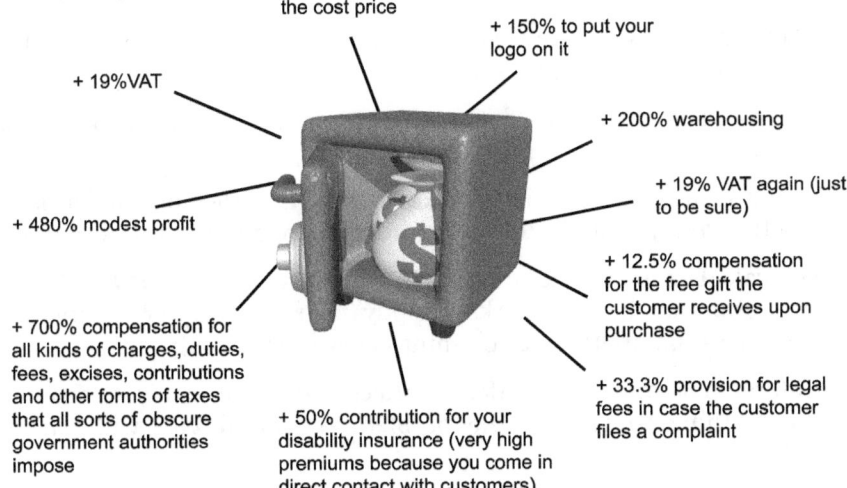

the cost price

+ 150% to put your logo on it

+ 19% VAT

+ 200% warehousing

+ 480% modest profit

+ 19% VAT again (just to be sure)

+ 12.5% compensation for the free gift the customer receives upon purchase

+ 700% compensation for all kinds of charges, duties, fees, excises, contributions and other forms of taxes that all sorts of obscure government authorities impose

+ 50% contribution for your disability insurance (very high premiums because you come in direct contact with customers)

+ 33.3% provision for legal fees in case the customer files a complaint

## Price ballet

A serious form of mental deviation is the fallacy that prices are fixed. To be sure, there are dozens of government agencies that want us to believe that. However, in practice, they are simply public employment projects, since a creative entrepreneur can always find hundreds of ways of using costs and prices to make customers' lives hell.

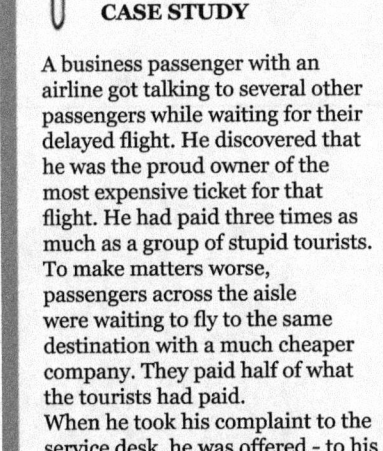

**CASE STUDY**

A business passenger with an airline got talking to several other passengers while waiting for their delayed flight. He discovered that he was the proud owner of the most expensive ticket for that flight. He had paid three times as much as a group of stupid tourists. To make matters worse, passengers across the aisle were waiting to fly to the same destination with a much cheaper company. They paid half of what the tourists had paid.

When he took his complaint to the service desk, he was offered - to his own dumbfounded surprise - a 75% refund on his ticket. He took the bait and hurried to the counter of the other airline company, who sold him a ticket dirt-cheap. He ended up with mud on his face when it appeared that the flight was overbooked and left without him. He did not get his money back because that was clearly stated in the general terms and conditions of the company. He ended up on his original flight, in first class, because business class was sold out. Meanwhile, he had paid **eight** times more for his ticket than the stupid tourists.

A selection of the usual practices:

---

✗ at the cash register, you charge the customer a higher amount than is stated on the price tag.;

✗ the price shown is only a down-payment, with 418 monthly payments to come;

✗ you indicate 'market price' and determine the price on the basis of whether or not you like the guy's mug (very popular in restaurants);

✗ you calculate a 'normal' price but add at least another 400% in 'costs' (for example: holiday parks happily charge extra for reservation costs, accommodation tax, cleaning costs, linens, etc.);

✗ different customers pay different prices and discover this, but cannot do anything to remedy the problem (standard fare with airline tickets);

✗ whenever you give 20% discount, you have first added 30% trading costs;

✗ you raise the prices of an article every week and simply stick the new price over the old, so that the customer can also follow the price evolution;

✗ you bill more than was agreed upon;

✗ you predate the invoice (say, by three months) and have the customer served with a subpoena.

---

## Summary

Price is emotional, and you can play on that freely. Nothing is so humiliating for the enemy as to realize that he has been 'had' and has paid more than family, friends, acquaintances and other customers, whom he then no longer dares to face.

GROUNDS FOR EXPULSION

**THE JERK FEELS LIKE HE HAS PAID A FAIR PRICE**

## 3. The Place
Proper selection of your battlefield will provide Chasers with distinct and lasting advantages.

| Places and channels for jerkering the enemy | |
| --- | --- |
| Channel/instrument | Tips: |
| **The Store**<br>Closed environment | • the customer is completely within your power, use that power to its fullest<br>• turn the store into a labyrinth<br>• ensure that no personnel are in sight |
| **At the customer's**<br>Surprise attack | • in theory this is a very stupid thing to do: why doesn't he come to you?<br>• barge in unexpectedly, even if you have an appointment<br>• do absolutely nothing after the meeting |
| **The home party**<br>For the advanced | • sell as much as possible; the spouse will ensure that you will never have to return again<br>• stay until after midnight chatting, and achieve the same effect |
| **The Internet**<br>Electronic highway | • make your website your only sales channel<br>• complicate the steps, so the client(s) cannot<br>• make no deliveries |
| **The telephone**<br>Call waiting (and waiting... and waiting) | • be unavailable (again)<br>• never place a call yourself<br>• let the customer wait for hours |
| **The fax**<br>Bermuda triangle | • the only faxes you send go to wrong numbers<br>• never pick up incoming faxes; they'll disappear by themselves |
| **Catalogue sales**<br>Window shopping only | • make the order form too small to fill out legibly<br>• have the jerks collect stamps to win non-existent prizes<br>• add at least 100 enclosures to create the utmost confusion possible |

Obviously, the best entertainment value is found in sending the enemy from pillar to post. Each sales channel should refer the enemy on to the next. If you can automate this process, you don't have to do anything yourself anymore. Then you have time for your real work

## The product is the deciding factor

The most notorious examples of customer cruelty, of course, stem from those organizations that have installed counters and front desks.

### CASE STUDY

Those who wish to secure a residence permit in Amsterdam – stupid foreigners, they should prevent people from doing their real work in their own country! – must report to the aliens registration department. At 8:00 am. At that time, the doors open for precisely one minute and the 40 people who will be processed that day are allowed to enter. The other 200 people may come back the next day to stand in line, which already starts forming at 4:00 am. Some spend the night there, if they're not chased away by the city police. Of the 40 'lucky' ones, at least three quarters are referred elsewhere because they lack one or another required document. In any case, no clients are allowed in the afternoon. What a paradise to work in!

More greatest hits:

- ✗ a sign on your storefront door stating "be right back", without giving a time;
- ✗ the notation "out of stock" on the website, while the product is still laying on the shelves in your store, and vice versa;
- ✗ ask your customer for the postal box address and then report that your delivery truck tried to make a delivery there in vain;
- ✗ placeyourmostpopularitemsattheback of the store, behind a long series of obstacles;
- ✗ demand the receipt for any returns, which, of course, you never gave the customer upon purchase of the item;

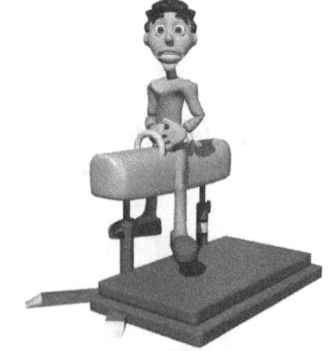

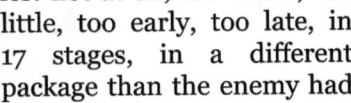

- ✗ personal contact offers unique opportunities, so ooze disinterest and cuss the jerk out whenever possible;
- ✗ help the jerk in the store when you have seven customers on hold on the phone and vice versa;
- ✗ make your deliveries: not at all, too much, too little, too early, too late, in 17 stages, in a different package than the enemy had requested, to the wrong address, with the wrong things, with the wrong invoice, with a double invoice;
- ✗ always be unavailable – wherever you are;
- ✗ everyday is Halloween so go for it: more trick than treat.

## Summary

'Place' means first and foremost that the jerk knows his/her place, and forces him/herself on you as little as possible. You take all the necessary precautions to make you and the desired products/services as inaccesible as possible.

GROUNDS FOR EXPULSION

THE CUSTOMER GETS HIS HANDS ON THE PRODUCT UNHINDERED

## 4. The P for Promotion

By 'promotion', Kotler refers to everything you do, with the use of advertisements, TV commercials, sponsoring, promotion, sales, mailings, samplings, special deals, etc., to make the following information known:

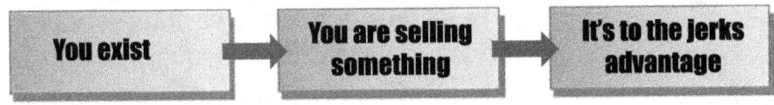

You exist ➤ You are selling something ➤ It's to the jerks advantage

Then, the enemy must be prompted to undertake the following steps:

Inquire ➤ Choose ➤ Buy ➤ Return

A completely senseless activity.

## The Box+:
## The Slow Demise of
## Great Expectations

If we assign the product or the service the collective term 'Box', then surrounding this Box is a 'Box+'. All the extras, which the jerk expects from you to make his life easier and more pleasant, can be indicated by this designation: easy to find out that you have the Box, how it works, how he can acquire it; easy to take home, to install and to use; easy to have replaced or fixed if something goes wrong.

The enemy employs the Law of Minimal Effort:

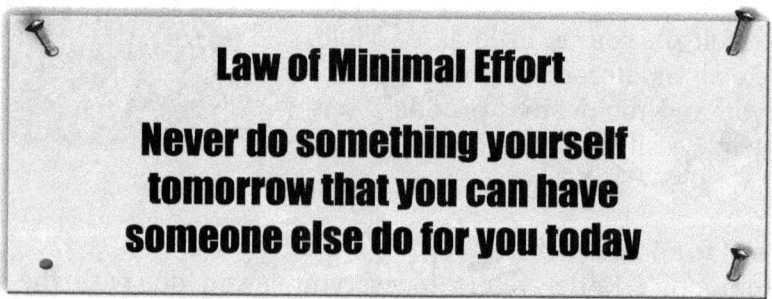

**Law of Minimal Effort**

**Never do something yourself
tomorrow that you can have
someone else do for you today**

The 'someone else' is you, of course, and that's why so much time is lost when dealing with customers.

In this you can include various services, extra-services, accessibility, quality and service guarantees, additional advantages, and all the trimmings, which only cost more of your valuable time.

Careful attention is called for, because the jerks are creatures of habit. Before you know it, they'll be addicted to all kinds of extras and can no longer see the forest for the trees.

You *can* sabotage the jerks expectations, little by little.

## Brainstorm

Fill out below at least 12 ways in which you can deny the customer every form of service and comfort. You can do this alone, or together in a brainstorming session with your colleagues. You have three minutes to complete this drill. Peeking ahead is not sporting.

| | |
|---|---|
| **1.** | |
| **2.** | |
| **3.** | |
| **4.** | |
| **5.** | |
| **6.** | |
| **7.** | |
| **8.** | |
| **9.** | |
| **10.** | |
| **11.** | |
| **12.** | |

We cannot emphasize the importance of the Box+ enough. If Sales have not been effective enough in keeping the enemy at bay, then Service (logistics, transport, administration, maintenance, the helpdesk, etc.) forms your **second chance**.

Speaking of helpdesks, here is the definition: A helpdesk is a desk behind which someone sits and, whenever the customer asks a question, yells "Help!!!". Just so.

## Badgering customers with non-service

There are literally millions of opportunities to raise the expectations of the enemy, and then fail to meet them. Some suggestions:

X try to find out early in the game what the enemy really wants, and then work as quickly as possible towards achieving the exact opposite;

X unobtrusively reduce the existing service package by charging a small fee for each (trans)action you complete (best example: banking transactions which used to be free). Employ the principles of fixing prices as described under the 2nd P above;

X make the instructions and conditions for services so obscure that the jerk never gets to use them;

X define various service levels and install a dart board to determine which jerk may benefit from which level;

X announce loudly that you provide extensive services, and then bring to the jerks attention the fact that he doesn't quite fall into the category of those who receive them.;

X use the natural talents in your organization to turn the simplest task into such a complex tangle that they no longer understand it themselves. Make a videotape of this and study it at home;

X set up a study group to map out during which phases of service the customer can be made to **wait**;

X automation will retard your services considerably and also make them substantially more expensive. Individual initiatives by employees (accidents will happen...) become impossible and the enemy must learn to reconcile him/herself to procedures which, very simply, differ from their wishes.

Formula for calculating the completion Time

$$t_c = t_n \times e_a \times 1/m_e$$

$t_c$ = completion time

$t_n$ = actual time necessary

$e_a$ = average percentage economized on services

$m_e$ = employees' mood)

There is another reason why Box+ is so important: customer expectations are increasing daily. Even the most hardened customer-fanatics are talking about the 'unsatisfiable customer', a reality that Club members realized a long time ago.

## Teamwork

Each organization has as many contact persons for providing services as there are employees. Thus, everyone must be involved in determining the liveable boundaries for customer service, preferably, in close teamwork.

### CASE STUDY

A company depended on e-mail for more than 75% of its turnover. When the company changed bank account, their ISP (Internet Service Provider) was informed by fax, with regard to the automatic direct debit for the subscription costs.

The ISP did not implement these changes, continued to fruitlessly collect their money, and added service charges each time, without ever notifying the company. After two (!) years the company suddenly received a 'last' (read: actually the first) final notice for the overdue amount for 1 year. The company paid promptly. The mailbox was closed down anyway.

The customer was asked by thetelephonic helpdesk three times (after waiting for more than three quarters of an hour each time) to fax their statement of payment. Finally, the helpdesk reported that another year had to be paid, - by e-mail, which the customer, of course, could not access. After two more phone calls the customer discovered the truth and again, promptly paid up. The mailbox was not reconnected because the administration first wanted to receive a new standing order by mail. Thereafter, the technical services took 48 hours before the mailbox was reactivated. The company had not received any e-mail for two weeks and was on the verge of bankruptcy.

A brilliant example of inter-departmental teamwork.

At a congress for customer service, one of the speakers, the manager of a large food manufacturer, gave a lecture on the quality of logistics and service. Someone in the audience asked why he didn't talk about the quality of the product itself. "Sorry," he answered, "I've forgotten it again. You see, we take that so for granted that we don't even think about it anymore.". Customers think exactly the same way. The product is a prerequisite for them. Suppliers are measured by their Box+ and the Box++. Herein lies your big chance!

## Summary

Life consists of a long succession of choices. Are you doing the customer a good turn or yourself? It is an inevitable, painful choice. It is either/or. It is also a choice between being social or antisocial: your decisions also determine the fate of your colleagues, who may or may not be then inundated with piles of work.

## The Box++: The Kingdom of Apathy

Surrounding the Box+ is yet another 'Box++'. This is the collective term for everything that you, **personally,** can add to all of the foregoing: your personal charisma, all the verbal and non-verbal signals that you give a customer, your 'personal performance'.

Box++ consists of three parts:

**Being pleasant**

Does the customer look forward to talking to you, or can he/she barely suppress his/her revulsion?

**Reliability**

Do you promise to do something, and do you then do what you have promised?

**Expertise**

Do you know what you are talking about?

It's obvious what you need to do: you must exude the exact opposite. Customers make decisions based on their impressions. The impression that you make determines their appreciation for the service(s) you provide. That appreciation, in turn, determines how they view your products. The Box++ is thus, the determinate of everything. Hence:

| You talk only about subjects you know nothing about | You are as unreliable as hell | Customers won't touch you with a ten-foot pole. |
| --- | --- | --- |

In short, you act like the model customer service employee.

## Brainstorm

Fill out below at least 12 ways in which you can thoroughly ruin the atmosphere for the customer. You can do this alone, or in a brainstorming session with your colleagues. You have three minutes to complete this task. Peeking ahead is unsporting.

| | |
|---|---|
| **1.** | |
| **2.** | |
| **3.** | |
| **4.** | |
| **5.** | |
| **6.** | |
| **7.** | |
| **8.** | |
| **9.** | |
| **10.** | |
| **11.** | |
| **12.** | |

Incidentally, the word 'pleasant' is derived from French and is related to *plaisanterie* (little joke) and *plaire* (to please others). In the world of customers this will lead to total catastrophe.

## Box++: the 'final touch'

The best advice we can give you is to follow your own feelings and instinct. Box++ is very personal and is based on your aptitude and improvisational talents. Nevertheless, a few illustrious examples:

| | |
|---|---|
| ✗ never say hello or goodbye; | ✗ never look the enemy directly in the eyes; |
| ✗ sound as uninterested as possible; exude non-verbally as much | ✗ make jokes about the customers within earshot; |
| ✗ aversion as possible; | ✗ never do what you have promised; |
| ✗ remove all emotion from your voice and sound as bored as possible, practice this every morning for 15 minutes with a tape recorder; | ✗ never tell the customer that there is a problem with his order until it's too late to do anything about it. |

## "It's a pleasure to do business there".

There are also agonizing examples in the land of chasing customers away. In the following example, one supplier has gotten the message, while the other makes one hopeless mistake after another.

CASE STUDY

The office manager of a company that used paper like it grew on trees was instructed by her director to place their orders for photocopy paper with supplier B instead of by A from then on. Both supplied the same products for the same price but the terms of payment with B were somewhat better. Less than a week later, the director heard her placing an order with company A.

"It's true," she said, as she went on to explain. "When I called B for information about a special kind of cardboard, I had to wait almost 10 minutes on the line, only to hear from a rude guy that he couldn't find the data and didn't have time to look for it. With A I didn't have to wait and they said they would call me back the same day. In less than an hour I had the information I needed."

Customers are just like people. People allow their emotions to dictate their actions. These emotions are your easiest target.

Never forget: any message you emit will have a contagious effect.

GROUNDS FOR EXPULSION

YOU SHOW A SMIDGEON OF ENTHUSIASM

## Awardability-factor

Box+ and Box++ together form the supplier's 'awardability-factor'.. Customers award or grant their supplier profit to the extent in which he/she meets the customer's expectations in these two areas. This is also a deciding factor in your working enjoyment. It determines the extent to which the customer, during those inevitable moments of contact, will be friendly on the phone, make many or few complaints, and consequently will eat up a lot or a little of your time.
Therefore, a high awardability-factor should be avoided like the plague. You don't even want to think about your customers getting attached to you!

**In summary, here are the basic principles:**

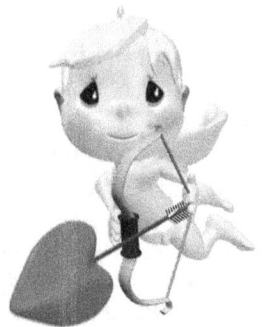

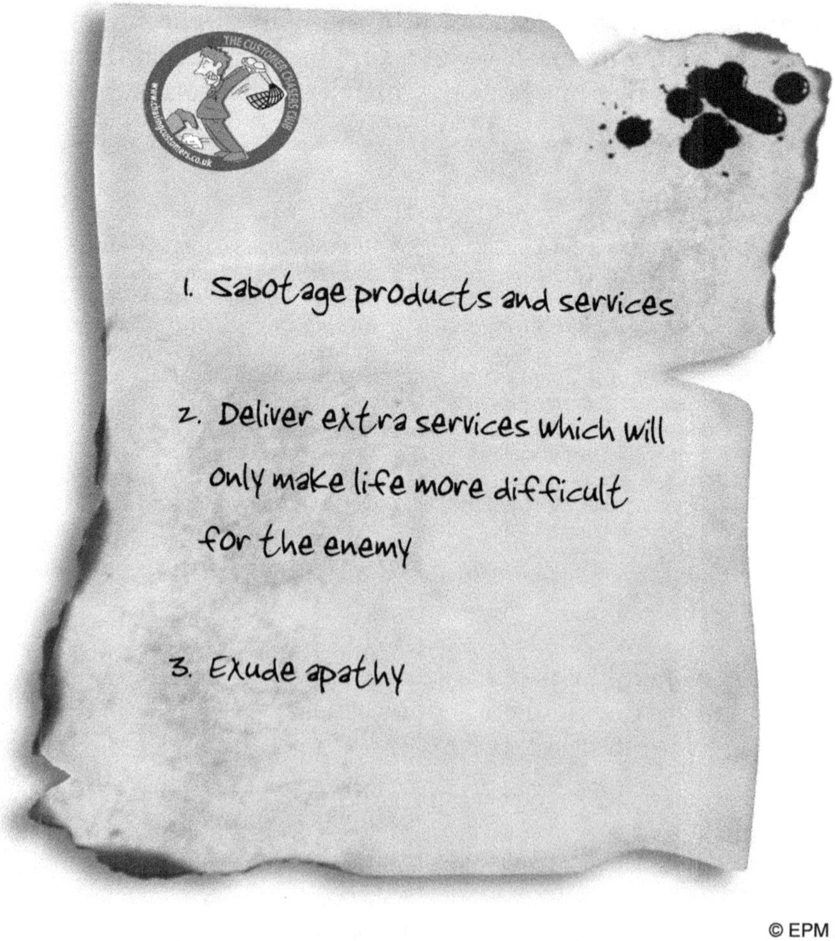
THE CUSTOMER CHASERS CLUB
www.chasingcustomers.co.uk
1. Sabotage products and services
2. Deliver extra services which will only make life more difficult for the enemy
3. Exude apathy

# Tactical Area of Attention # 1:
# The Telephone

Every organization has an extensive telephonic infrastructure: fixed telephones, cell phones, pagers, sometimes even satellite telephones. The idea is to be as accessible as possible; you can chat with your colleagues at any time. The enemy abuses this infrastructure large-scale, however, in order to infiltrate the organization and severely impair your working enjoyment. On average, you conduct at least thirty telephone conversations daily, either with customers or on their behalf. A simple calculation clearly illustrates the kind of catastrophic consequences this has, not only for the entertainment value of your job, but also for the cost-effectiveness of your organization.

"The telephone, without a doubt, eats up the most time within every organization!"

| Example: | |
|---|---|
| Number of employees: | 50 x |
| Number of calls daily: | 30 x |
| Number of working days annually: | 200 |
| Number of calls annually: | 300.000 |

There is only one thing to do: eradicate this phenomenon. You must reclaim your infrastructure and once again become master of your own time, captain of your own calling-conglomerate. Immediate action is required regarding the following three strategic objectives.

## Strategic Objective A: distribution of telephone numbers.

Subversive elements surreptitiously help the jerks by disclosing your telephone number at every opportunity: on business cards, in advertisements, on the Internet, in brochures, yes, even in telephone books. It is imperative that you take action, either by stopping the circulation of these numbers completely or at least by distributing incorrect telephone numbers.

Travel Agency "Intergalactic" Ltd.

A.T. Yoorsurvis
Helpdesk Manager, International Travels

Telephone: 1-800-Ambulance

Moreover, the telephone is the most difficult, and the most versatile communication instrument. It's a two-way street:

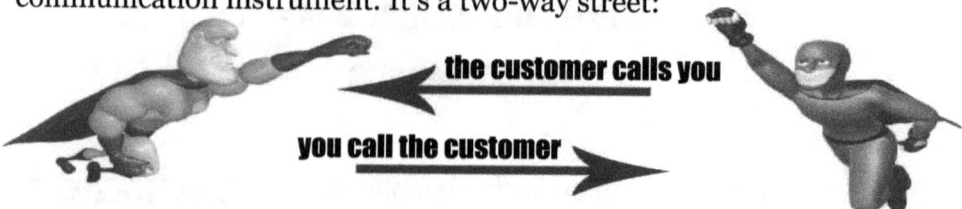

**the customer calls you**

**you call the customer**

Because this makes elimination of the enemy doubly difficult, you must have a battle plan laid out in order to attack these two fronts simultaneously.

### Strategic Objective B: You call the customer

This is, of course, the very worst thing you can possibly do. it is sufficient grounds to have you banned from the Customer-Chasers Club for your lifetime and several of your descendants.

Contacting the customer - for **any** reason - is **strictly prohibited!** It doesn't matter if your cat is on fire and your customer has the only extinguisher in the city. It doesn't matter if the earth is about to be struck by an enormous comet and your customer has a spaceship. You may not call them **for any reason!** This is war - maintain total radio silence. Of course, you are still required to promise to call the customer - but never ever do it. Never. Ever. If you are in the sales field or an attorney, you are already proficient in this area. Congratulations!

Keep setting the bar for the rest of us. Once freed from your cellular chains, imagine the time you will free up for really important things like meals and relationships! The cost savings are another bonus - we have testimony from the Customer Chaser who saved, in one year, enough money to actually pay his taxes.

### Strategic Objective C: The customer calls you

State legislatures have tried to outlaw this practice; the Supreme Court has reviewed countless briefs - to no avail. Customers are going to call you. It is the most pernicious, vicious and malicious strategy in their arsenal - and they use it gleeful impunity. There you are, quietly and ambitiously going about your work when the phone rings. Unsolicited - unwarranted. On the other end of the line is a customer with a question you've answered for them several hundred times this month.

Whenever a customer calls, pretend you are on your other line with a "really important" customer. For those who persist in calling you, program the longest voice mail outgoing message ever conceived - 9 min. at least. If they're going to bother you, make them really pay for it.

With some difficulty, you control your rage and answer the question yet again - but it's too late. The damage has already been done to your psyche, soul and health - because you know, in your heart of hearts, that same customer will call back by end of day.

Your situation has become a matter of self defense! Legally, any means you employ to defend yourself are justified. When customers call you with their innumerable stories, problems ans excuses, you must take control using tactical guidelines to repel the enemy. The Strategic Objective can be split into a short and long-term illustration:

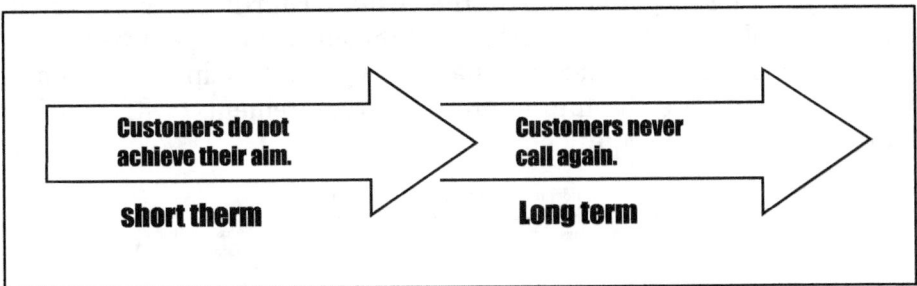

Your approach to their calls must be so drastic that the customer will think twice, or three times, before he calls you again. The quality of

your irritation on the call is as important as the quantity of frustration you display. Employ as many diversionary tactics as possible - so that the customer hangs up without achieving his goal. Also, if you have a receptionist or switchboard - it's time to start bribing the gatekeeper to fulfill their function.

## The ultimate weapon: silence is golden

'You scratch my back and I'll scratch yours' is the motto of every customer. You can frustrate customers optimally by having them invest the maximum effort without producing any results. On the telephone, this can best be achieved through silence - endless, cut-to-the-quick silence.

A measurable target can be set: 95% of the time that customers spend on the phone, they wait in silence for ......, actually they have no idea, but they sit and they wait. Simon & Garfunkel scored a mega-hit in the sixties with it, and you can score on the telephone everyday with it, too: The Sounds of Silence.

## Your arsenal of weapons

He (or she) who possesses the proper and perfectly maintained materials and munition has already won half the battle. So always look after your equipment religiously. Customers will catch you unawares at the most unexpected moments and then you won't have time to look for the necessary gear. Your workplace is the nerve center of all your activities. Organize it then, as *your* fort, according to *your* taste and *your* rules. The worst thing that can happen is that subversive elements – such as colleagues collaborating with the enemy – can find things during your absence and so help the customer further. You, yourself, should be able to withstand the temptation during phone conversations to have documents within reach that could possible help the customer. Therefore, here are the minimum, basic requirements, with which a workplace should be equipped:

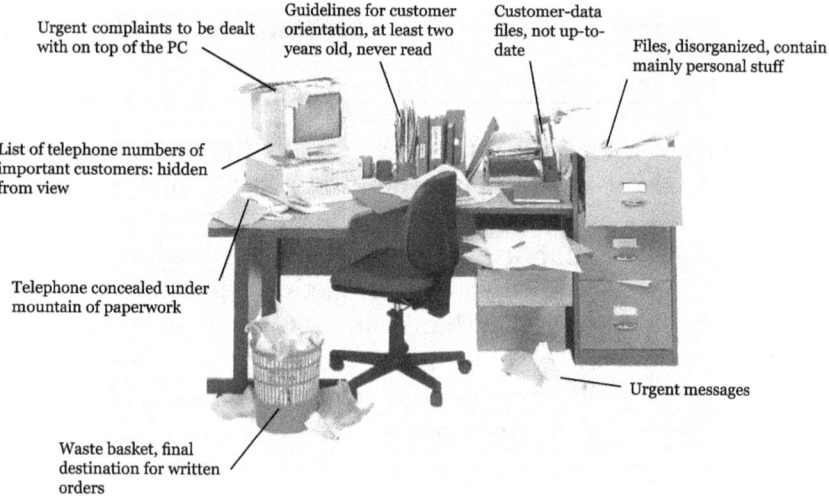

Urgent complaints to be dealt with on top of the PC

Guidelines for customer orientation, at least two years old, never read

Customer-data files, not up-to-date

Files, disorganized, contain mainly personal stuff

List of telephone numbers of important customers: hidden from view

Telephone concealed under mountain of paperwork

Waste basket, final destination for written orders

Urgent messages

Furthermore, the following checklist will help you keep a good inventory of weapons at hand:

| Do not have | Have |
|---|---|
| Sharpened pencils | All sorts of food |
| Pens that write | Cups of coffee (spillable!!) |
| Note pad | Open newspaper (rustles!) |
| Customer-data files | Crocheting and knitting (also audible) |
| Supply lists | Internal telephone numbers (transfer to someone else!) |
| Agenda | Radio |
| Cough syrup | Tape recorder with background noise |
| Keyboard (hidden under piles) | Colleague talking loudly |
| Network connection for the PC | Answering machine |
| *Complete further on your own:* | *Complete further on your own:* |
| | |

## Brainstorm

| | |
|---|---|
| **1.** | Fill out below at least 12 techniques designed to harass the customer on the telephone. You can do this alone or in a brainstorming session with your colleagues. You have three minutes to complete this task. Peeking ahead is unsporting. |
| **2.** | |
| **3.** | |
| **4.** | |
| **5.** | |
| **6.** | |
| **7.** | |
| **8.** | |
| **9.** | |
| **10.** | |
| **11.** | |
| **12.** | |

## Techniques

The defense against incoming phone calls consists of four ramparts. Each wall represents an attempt to block a conversation, or prevent the jerk from chieving his goal.

When building each of these walls, you can deploy a number of different techniques:

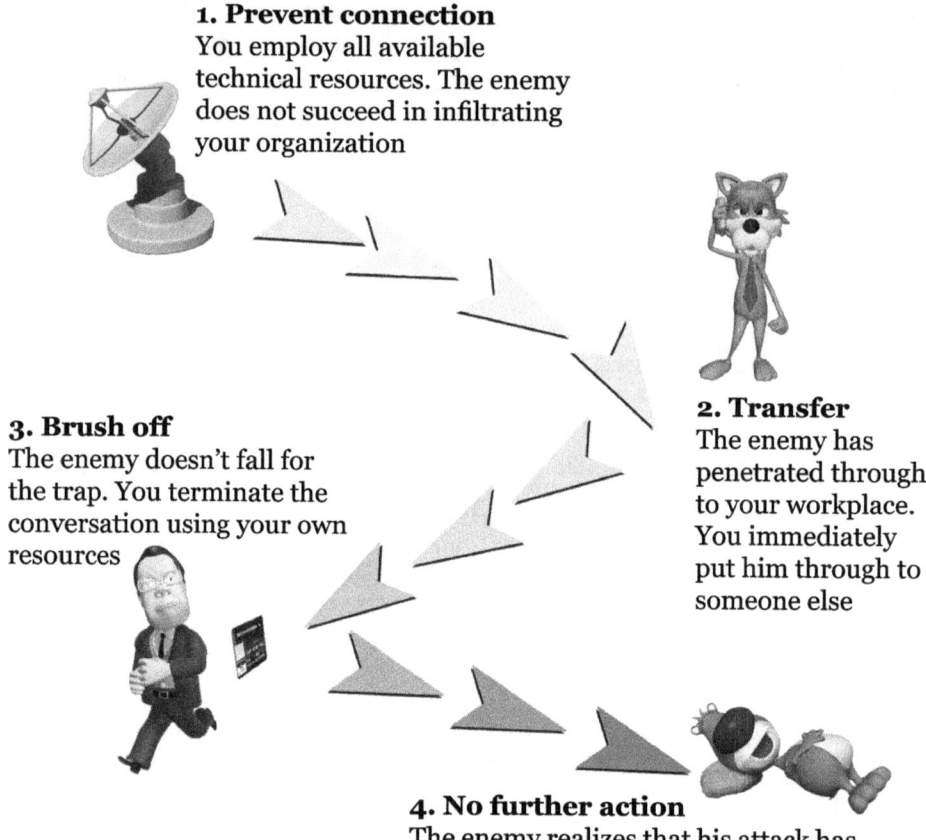

### 1. Prevent connection
You employ all available technical resources. The enemy does not succeed in infiltrating your organization

### 2. Transfer
The enemy has penetrated through to your workplace. You immediately put him through to someone else

### 3. Brush off
The enemy doesn't fall for the trap. You terminate the conversation using your own resources

### 4. No further action
The enemy realizes that his attack has been foiled: nothing happens

## Prevent connection

Conducting phone calls with the customer is an ambiguous activity. On the one hand, the jerks on the phone eat up most of your time; on the other hand, much enjoyment can be experienced by ill-treating the initially unsuspecting victims. You can sharpen your intellectual skills by thwarting their cunning attempts to put you to work. With each victory, you will acquire   subject material for the next team meeting.

**Give moral support to your inexperienced colleagues. Point out the great entertainment value of desperate customers**

Throughout this interaction, you, yourself, are in no danger at all since the enemy cannot in any way inflict any bodily harm. However, a small warning must be issued at this time: psychological warfare with the enemy can be very intense at times. Thus, it is recommended that you not leave inexperienced colleagues to fend for themselves. You should remind them regularly of the long-term objective, "Get rid of the customer!" and of the great entertainment value to be had from telephone conversations with desperate customers.

In short, you decide for yourself if you want to take the time for phone calls, or if you want to preclude them right from the start. The simplest, but also the most effective technique is quite obvious - you simply disconnect the phone. There are two variations here. You do this just once in the morning when you arrive and restore the connection when you leave your workplace, or you do this whenever the phone rings. The latter is very labor-intensive, but the rewards are that much greater: You don't need much fantasy to imagine the increasing frustration of the helpless, unsuccessful enemy!

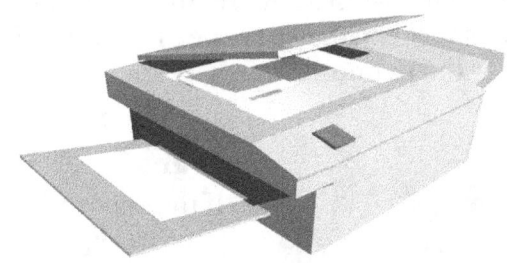

Another variation is switching the telephone and fax-machine plugs. The customer will get an earsplitting screech at each attempt and will finally give up of his own accord after a time. By the way, this is the only reason why you should still have a fax-machine in your office. Just as fascinating, albeit rather aggravating for your working environment, is **not** answering the phone. You simply let it ring. And ring. And ring. Once again, you run absolutely no risk. It has been scientifically proven: statistics show that the ringing stops sooner or later.

As an alternative you could also pick up the receiver and then hang up immediately. It confuses the enemy to no end and - it costs money!

Since there's a good chance the same jerk will call back several times in a row, it is great fun to alternate the last two techniques. The customer first doesn't get through, and then is briefly connected, only to hear a dial tone again.

The use of an answering machine is highly recommended, obviously, but is subject to several conditions:

- ✗ the machine is - preferably - turned on during office hours as well;
- ✗ the recorded message is barely intelligible;
- ✗ the message contains almost no information, certainly not about when you *can* be reached (if you are, indeed, available at all);
- ✗ the customer can leave a message after the beep, but there is no beep;
- ✗ the message does not get recorded so that you are not tempted to respond to it.

*... for the voicemail of J. Smith, dial 76, for the voicemail of P. Baker, dial 77. If you really insist on speaking to someone personally, please try again on the third Friday of the month between 12 minutes after 8 and 28 minutes before 9.*

Especially irritating and, therefore highly recommendable, is the use of the answering machine after the customer has gotten through a number of times and so thinks that the end is in sight. A particularly rewarding variation is a telephone with voicemail-function. In the meantime, you ensure that the customer is footing the bill for the phone costs.

### Transfer

If the enemy does manage to penetrate through to your workplace, it's then a question of getting rid of him a.s.a.p.. This technique is called 'transfer'.

Using finely tuned teamwork, you should ensure that the client keeps getting transferred until he throws in the towel himself. Six transferals is minimum, with the exception of complaints. Complaints have such a great entertainment value that it would be a sin to keep them from the rest of the organization. Moreover, you must agree amongst yourselves who will handle the complaint first, because the more often the jerk repeats his story, the shorter it gets. It would not be fair if it were always the same colleagues who were allowed to enjoy the long version. So, – take turns!

**Tip**
**Taking a telephone hostage: "One moment, please!" followed by • silence**

Ensure that you always connect someone to the **right person**. The right person is the colleague who does **not** know the answer to the customer's inquiry. The person who does know how to respond must be carefully kept out of the way.

*Before* you transfer someone, you emphasize the total inanity of the customer by asking the question "What **was** your name **again** ...?". The jerk is given the feeling that he has no name, that he doesn't count, that he's a nobody. The correct conclusion.

When transferring, you say, "One moment, please!" to the customer. There is technical term for this: **telephone hostage**.

What is a telephone hostage? It is someone who:

- ✗ has been robbed of his freedom – the customer cannot leave the telephone because you could (theoretically) return any moment;

- ✗ cannot do anything to remedy the situation himself – the customer can shout "hello..?!" as often as he wants and nothing will happen anyway;

- ✗ doesn't know how long it will take;

- ✗ meanwhile, has access to little or no food or drink.

Next, you let the enemy sit and stew for 15 to 20 minutes. Then you listen again to see if he/she is still on the line. If that is the case, you must act very quickly.

You ask "Are you still there?", then, without pausing, add "One moment!" and you let the customer wait again. Repeat until it is silent on the other end.

If so desired, you can make use of background music – the so-called Muzak. Gratifying tunes are house, country & western, Mantovani or electronic versions of worn-out Classic FM winners.

In the best scenario, the person to whom you were going to put the customer through is also unavailable. Studies are frequently done into the availability of the average office employee:

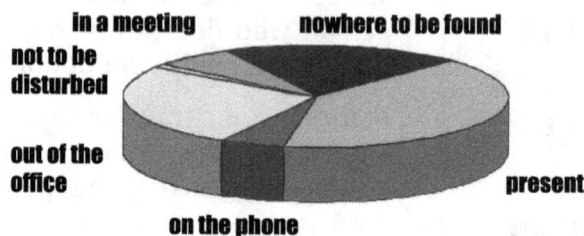

in a meeting     nowhere to be found

not to be disturbed

out of the office     present

on the phone

source: Quentel

The above pie chart illustrates that approximately 40% of the working population still doesn't get it: they are simply available for phone calls! Unbelievable.

The other 60% have figured it out because they are:

- ✗ on the phone. Never say this directly to a customer. The correct expression is: "Mr. X is in the office, but I cannot put you through, because he is talking to a very **important** customer. (A persistent enemy who has not yet figured it out);
- ✗ not in the office: "visiting an **important** customer", etc.:
- ✗ not to be disturbed;
- ✗ in a meeting;
- ✗ and the best of them all: nowhere to be found.

In this last instance, an enthralling conversation is acted out:

     Good morning, this is Y. Could I please speak to X?

No. [*]

     Oh, is he not in the office?

Yes, he is.

     Is he in a meeting?

No, he's not.

     What's the matter, then?

[You can hear yourself saying it, right?:] He's not at his desk!

     Couldn't you look for him?

Hah, look for X, he could be anywhere.

     Well, yes, but can't you page him?

Yes, but he never calls back anyway.

     What should I do then?

What do you think?

     Uh...... call back tomorrow?

Great idea! Goodbye. [click]

---

(*) The jerk started it. We're not going to help him, right? Let him figure it out himself!

## Brush-off

If you really don't succeed in obstructing the enemy or passing him off, then you'll just have to finish the job yourself.

A modest choice from the hundreds of techniques you could utilize:

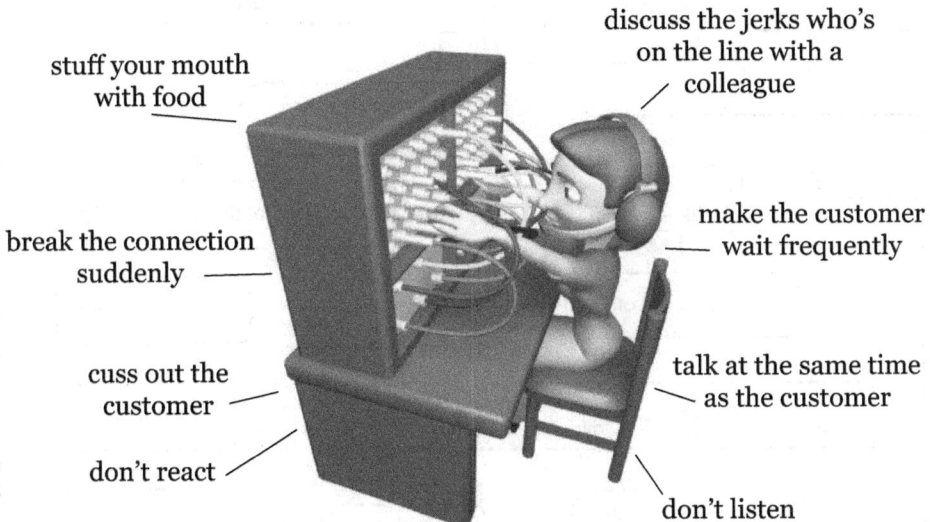

stuff your mouth with food

discuss the jerks who's on the line with a colleague

break the connection suddenly

make the customer wait frequently

cuss out the customer

talk at the same time as the customer

don't react

don't listen

With any of these options, you determine the duration of the conversation. If you lack time or have had enough, one click is sufficient to get you back to doing interesting things.

## No further action

The enemy assumes that his attack will yield some results and that what he/she has requested and/or what you have promised will actually come to pass. Either the little bugger expects action (but you do absolutely nothing) or he assumes you will return his call (but you don't). That would be contrary to Strategic Objective B: **Never** call the customer.

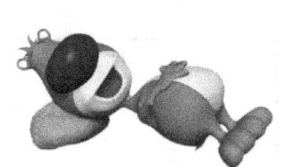

On the next page, a clear battle plan is laid out. Commit it to memory.

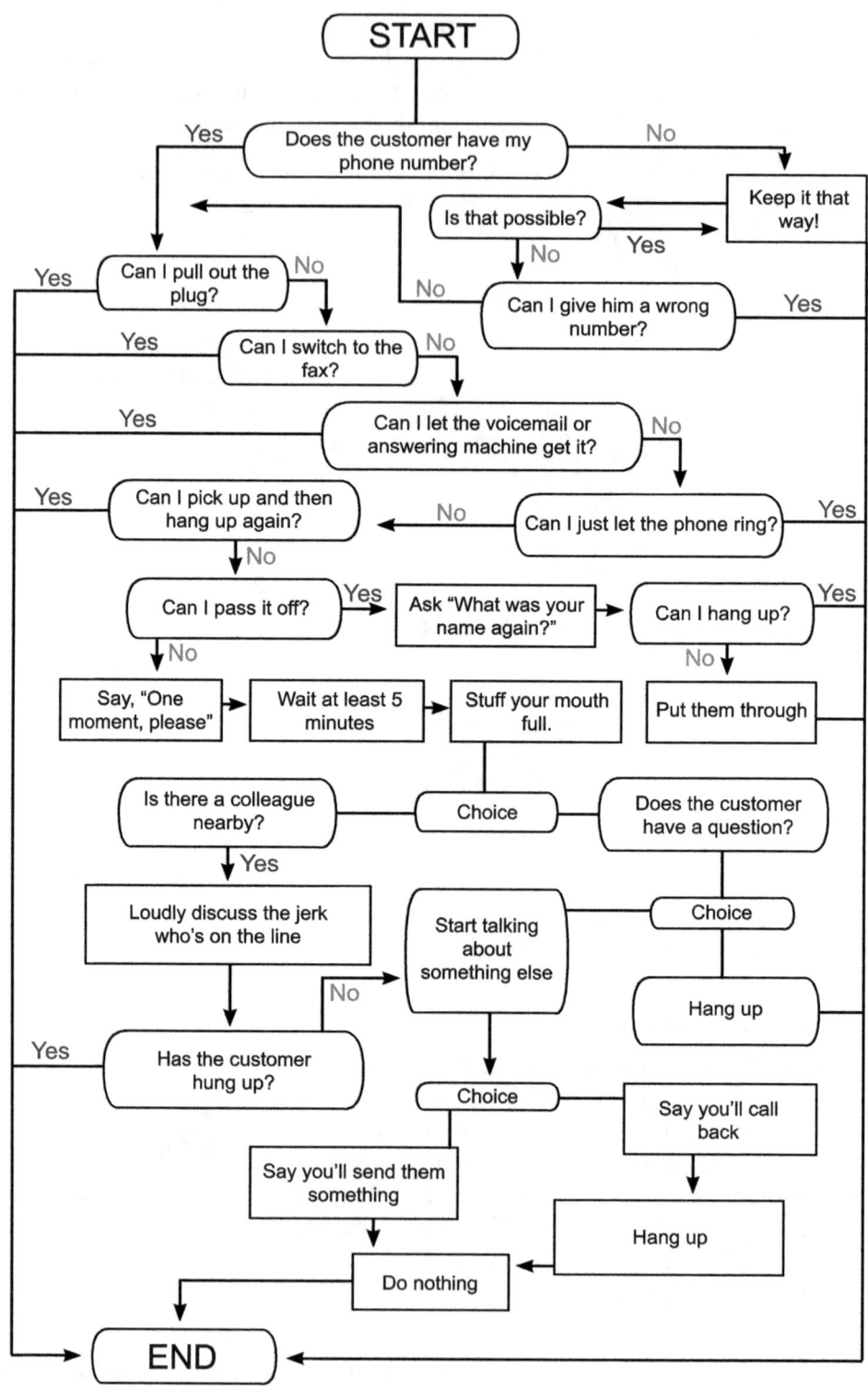

© EPM 2009

## Tactical Area of Attention # 2:
## The personal conversation

## "The personal conversation is without a doubt the most dangerous form of contact with a customer!"

A personal conversation with a customer or potential customer is the worst thing that can happen to you: it could lead to a transaction. It could mean a purchase, an order, an assignment, a question about maintenance, a repair job or a request: the list of customer expectations unfortunately is endless. Whatever the customer wants at a given moment, the inevitable result is always that employees from your organization will have to get down to work, and they already have their hands full with their *real* work. Just imagine: you return from a meeting with one of those jerks and you have to explain to your colleagues, who wait with baited breath, that the enemy has gotten his way, that they will be deprived long-term of the time to do their own work, and particularly, deprived of their job satisfaction ... and it's all your fault.

GROUNDS FOR EXPULSION

YOU ALLOW THE TRANSACTION TO BE COM— PLETED.

Your social downfall is complete. You don't dare show your face at work for weeks on end. You call in sick. You are no longer invited to any parties, and in the company cafeteria you are glared at. No one will sit beside you on the company outing, and you can forget a promotion altogether. You are destined to go through life as an outcast.

It all boils down to preventing the customer from signing on the dotted line at all costs. For this reason, many companies frequently have their best employees working out in the field. After all, the risks are immense and the interests, enormous. However, chasing your customers away through personal conversations is also a question of teamwork. Whenever you are aware that a colleague is standing face to face with the enemy, you are expected to come to his or her rescue. More about this later.

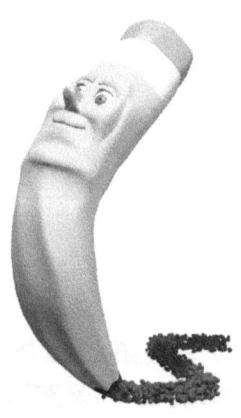

The sixty-four-thousand dollar question is: should you avoid meeting with customers at all costs, or rather, take advantage of the opportunity to give them such a severe dressing-down as to ensure that they will never dream of doing business with your organization again? Your best entertainment value lies in leading a conversation that, for the customer, progresses in the most excruciatingly inefficient and ineffective manner. This is the highest good. You should try to exercise this option whenever possible.

Whether or not you can exercise this option depends upon the following conditions: that you possess the necessary skills to play with the customer as a cat plays with a mouse, and that you can afford to spend the time.

The following figure will help you to decide:

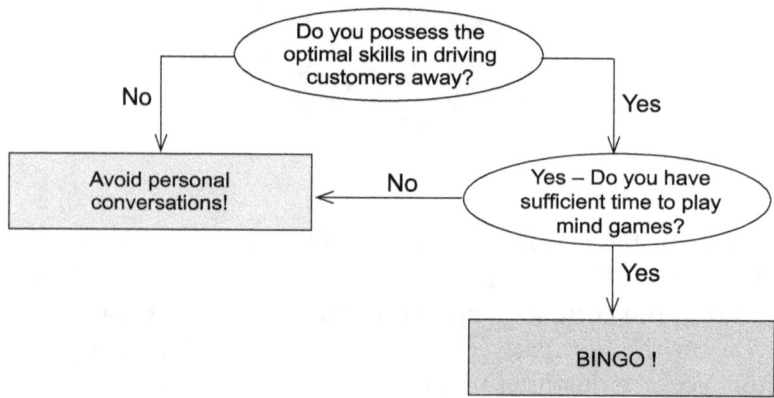

## Two strategies, two tactics

On a strategic level, you need to differentiate between two separate strategies: you can go to the customer yourself, or you can have the customer come to you. Moreover, there are two tactics from which you can choose:. These together lead to four types of confrontations with the customer:

|  | The customer comes | You go there |
|---|---|---|
| **By appointment** | Abuser's paradise | Into the lion's den |
| **Spur of the moment** | impertinence | Surprise attack |

As this confrontation matrix indicates, you are always playing with fire during a personal conversation! You must have a decisive, well-prepared policy and implementation. For this reason, these four confrontation types are examined more closely below.

## Strategic perspective A:

You have the customer come to you. At first this sounds like stupidity to the nth degree. Harassing your customers until they leave – of course!

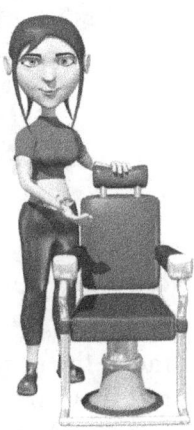

But inviting the enemy into your own biotope? Come on!You may only invite a customer into your domain if you're absolutely sure of what you're doing, and you can guarantee your colleagues that no work, inconvenience or trials and tribulations will emanate from this customer contact. This approach also has some advantages:

- ✗ when you invite a customer onto your own turf, you can be certain that you yourself control all of the elements. The customer can hardly surprise you with colleagues who unexpectedly join the meeting, or with conference rooms where your cell phone has no coverage, etc.;

- ✗ you can work under the ideal conditions: you have lured the enemy into an enclosed space and you can do

- ✗ whatever you want, no Peeping Toms. The customer has nowhere to hide, he must endure whatever you subject him to, and

- ✗ you need not invest your traveling time.

Through all of this, we are assuming that you have invited the customer yourself, and have scheduled an suitable appointment. It's something entirely different if a customer suddenly spontaneously, unannounced and very sneakily appears on your doorstep. This sort of impertinence must be punished adequately: the customer must not get that for which he has come, and it should cost him at least triple the time that he has available.

Many organizations have designated special areas where the unannounced jerks can go: stores and service counters. There, the enemy can be observed with cameras, the interior is designed use every opportunity for harassment possible, and highly-trained, specialized staff are present.

The motto:

**They're in?**

**Get rid of 'em as fast as you can!**

### Strategic perspective B: You go to the customer

This means that you are prepared to invest considerable amounts of time in the customer contact: traveling time + meeting time + traveling time. You are now balancing on the edge of accountability. A bigger investment must of course yield an even bigger profit. Returning to the

office with your sole accomplishment being that the customer's intended transaction has not been fulfilled is not sufficient. You can only be completely satisfied with yourself if the customer never, EVER wants to do business with your organization again. You should realize that you are entering the lion's den here. The customers have all of the strategic advantages on their side. This can only be avoided by launching a surprise attack: you show up announced (or, perhaps, a day too early).

## Brainstorm

Fill out below at least 12 techniques designed to harass your customers into leaving, using either an appointment or a personal conversation. You can do this alone or have a brainstorming session with your colleagues. You have three minutes to complete this task. Looking ahead is unsporting.

| | |
|---|---|
| **1.** | |
| **2.** | |
| **3.** | |
| **4.** | |
| **5.** | |
| **6.** | |
| **7.** | |
| **8.** | |
| **9.** | |
| **10.** | |
| **11.** | |
| **12.** | |

## Your arsenal of weapons:

He (or she) who possesses the correct and perfectly maintained materials and munition has already won half the battle. So give your constant attention to your equipment. Customers will surprise you at the most unexpected moments and then you won't have time to look for the necessary gear.

Furthermore, the following checklist will help you keep a good inventory of weapons at hand:

| Do not have at hand | Have at hand |
|---|---|
| Customer's address | Other customer's data |
| Customer's telephone number | Irrelevant material |
| Directions | Cell phone (turned on) |
| Customer's name | Garlic spray |
| General customer data | Another file to peruse while you |
| Notes on previous conversations | are talking to the customer |
| Preparation for the meeting | |
| Relevant documents | *Complete further on your own:* |
| Relevant samples | |
| | |
| *Complete further on your own:* | |

## Techniques

The best defense Techniques against any possible transactions is divided into three stages of battle. Each stage meets the requirements in an attempt to avoid meeting with the customer, or at least, to prevent it from yielding any results:

✗ advance guard fighting: preparing for a conversation;

✗ combat: the battle itself;

✗ rearguard action: the after "care".

## Advance guard fighting:
## Preparing for the conversation.

An ounce of prevention is worth a pound of cure. Being well prepared is half the battle. Forewarned is forearmed. You know all the platitudes, and if there is *one* situation where you should take heed, it is here!

Remember: all of your colleagues are counting on you! Your skillful handling of this frontal attack by the enemy will fulfill their dreams – or not. You can do a great deal in the advance guard to block the customer *before* he ever really gets going.

Your most important ally is your agenda. It's full, packed, or simply lost. A mere smattering of the many possibilities:

- ✗ "I would like to make an appointment with you but I can't find my agenda. I'll call you back tomorrow." (This does go against one of the most important telephone principles.);
- ✗ "We are working with a new electronic agenda but our computer system is down **again.**";
- ✗ "When you would like to meet? Oh no, I have absolutely no time for you before the end of next year.";
- ✗ "The only free slot in my agenda is on Friday evening at 6:30 pm, just after another appointment. Could we meet in Philadelphia?" (while your customer's office is in Houston or Atlanta);
- ✗ (should you for some silly reason call the customer yourself to make an appointment:) "Can you meet next Tuesday, since I'll be in your neighborhood then anyway." (gives the customer a wonderful feeling of importance);
- ✗ "You'll need to speak to my colleague about that." (customer: "Ok, but the last time you were helping me?" – you again : "well yeah, ......");
- ✗ "We only deal with those sorts of matters on the phone.";
- ✗ You make a memo of the appointment, which you then throw away immediately.

If you have still been unsuccessful in avoiding an appointment, you should plant the seed of disaster already during the preparation, which will as yet ensure that the meeting will not take place.

A few suggestions:

✗ you create confusion about the location of the meeting and ensure that your customer will show up at your office while you are at his. This produces fascinating telephone conversations;

Where are you?
Here!
   Yes, but weren't you supposed to
That's what I said.
   I mean here, not there!
Why?
   Because that's what we agreed on.
Says who?
   It's written in my agenda.
Well that's your problem.
   etc.

✗ you create confusion over the time of the appointment and ensure that the jerk arrives an hour early (+an hour for traffic jams makes for a nice total of wasted time). Or too late, so you can smilingly inform him/her that you are already well into your next appointment;
✗ you confirm the appointment in writing, with a subtle change to the place and/or time, for example: 2:40 pm instead of 4:20 pm.

Suppose that this is all for naught, then you have no recourse but to actually go ahead with the appointment with the customer. Go to your meeting with the customer well prepared. For example, this could entail:

✗ you do not prepare at all for the actual content of the meeting;
✗ you do not have anything with you that could even remotely be useful during the conversation;
✗ you do have a huge pile of important-looking documents with you that have absolutely nothing to do with the subject at hand; and/or you have information with you regarding
✗ the opposite of what your customer wants; you send no directions of how to get to your office, or something cryptic;
✗ and/or you send them too late;

✗ whenever you go to the customer yourself, throw the directions to the office in the round file before you leave;

✗ of course, you have your cell phone with you – batteries fully charged.

And finally, a word of advice on your cuisine for the night before: garlic.

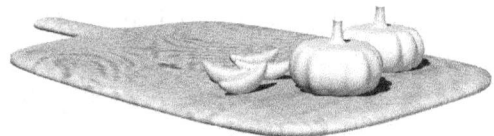

## The combat:
## During the battle

You are now sitting opposite the customer. The subtle game can begin: in the most refined manner possible you attempt to give the customer the feeling that he/she will eventually reach their final objective. The longer you can sustain this feeling, the bigger the disappointment - or rage – and the more likely that you will be delivered from this jerk

permanently. After a lengthy build-up of tension, the moment arrives in the conversation that the hopeful key question is posed: "So you can deliver this within the timeframe proposed?" You respond coolly, "No!", followed by an icy silence. The customer has been flattened with one move and is down for the count from your sledgehammer blow. You have won. This is close combat in its purest form.

A few techniques designed to slowly heighten the tension and to test the patience of the enemy:

✗ you don't show up at all, and have someone call to inform the customer when you should have already been there;

✗ you don't call at all;

✗ you come at least 15 minutes late with the announcement: "Sorry I'm a little late, but I've just had an appointment with an *important* customer that ran overtime.";

✗ you mention, of course, that you got caught in traffic (even if the jerk's office is around the corner from your own, and, for the truly talented: even if the customer has come to you;

- ✗ you sit with your back to the sun so that the customer continually has to look into the glaring sunlight during the meeting;
- ✗ you ask the customer if he objects to smoking, and, if that's the case, you hold the meeting in a smoke-filled conference room;
- ✗ you mention that a colleague will be joining you shortly and fill at least the next half hour with chit-chat while the colleague of course, never does show up for the meeting;
- ✗ alternatively: you bring five colleagues along who all work on the enemy simultaneously;
- ✗ you particularly do *not* listen to the jerk and ensure that you yourself are always talking;
- ✗ you speak with your mouth full (at least with candy, a complete lunch is better);
- ✗ you talk exclusively about the wonderful qualities of your products and services, and not about the advantages that they could provide the enemy;
- ✗ you make good use of the time by going over other documents and by signing outgoing mail;
- ✗ you have cold coffee served (in dirty cups), or none at all. As far as tea goes, there is only one flavor available (dishwater);
- ✗ under the guise of teamwork your colleagues call you continually, whereupon you always say that it's a very *important* phone call;
- ✗ finally, you leave early for an *important* appointment.

### Rear guard action: The after "care" after the meeting

What do you do after the meeting? You are unavailable for calls and only send him/her something when the jerk starts threatening to call his lawyers. Of course, then you send the wrong documents and/or the wrong written account of the meeting. After a time, I guarantee the customer will give up.

## Other tactical areas of attention: The Customer Chasers Club will not let you down !

There are a few billion active customers on this earth. Let us assume that each one of them annoys a supplier at least 10 times a year. This little calculation undoubtedly has just discouraged you from going to work tomorrow at all. Unfortunately, the creativity and perseverance of the enemy are infinite, and their numbers countless.

Dear members, do not give up too quickly, and remember that jerkering customers can also be your greatest source of working enjoyment:

A DAY WITHIHOUT PESTERING CUSTOMERS IS LIKE A DAY WITHOUT SUNSHINE

Make it into an office party:

X find the naturally-talented in your organization, make video-recordings of them at work and study them intently;

X learn from each other;

X set up little competitions: who can transfer a customer the most often, avoid eye contact as long as possible, send the biggest e-mails possible;

X offer prizes for the best ideas;

X etc.

## Advice

While enjoying this creative play, do NOT allow yourself to be lulled into a false sense of security. Remain vigilant and wary. Customers are known to lure you into actual transactions with all sorts of misleading ploys: money, sales, recognition, cheese, etc. There is no difference between a driveling, sniveling customers and any other – they all want part of your soul. Do not become distracted

– every customer is bad news. And all that glitters is not gold. If you're over your head, you can just as easily drown in champagne as water. Win one for the Gripper.

Our goal is to save you from the evil that lurks around your every business corner. While we have attempted to provide as much information and strateegy possible, we have only scratched the surface of your Customer Chasing options. The rest is up to you!

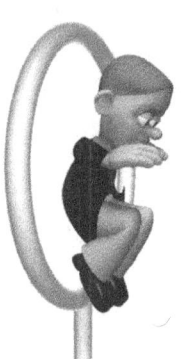

## Trick for Treats

Many Customer Chasing techniques are intended to trick the customer into doing what you want them to do – instead of you doing what they want you to do – do be do be doo. It is your job to *get them* to jump through the hoops. With each hoop, more pests will give up, leaving you to accomplish some real work. Turn hoop jumping into an internal competition – which of your colleagues needs the least amount of hoop to drive off their customers?

Manufacturer's Warranty: For most customer/pest problems, just one of the techniques outlined in this book will be necessary to achieve full and complete alienation. For more acute emergencies, our Customer Chasing consultants will be ready to assist in your every need.

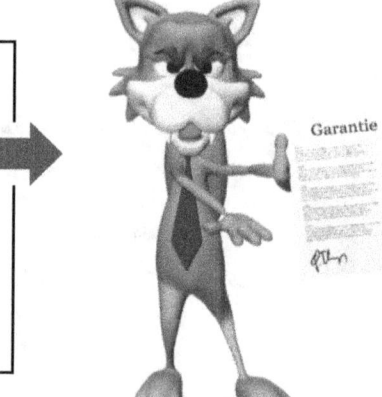

Garantie

## Your Future is Bright!

A little effort, creativity, dedication, chasing techniques, tenacity and cheese – these are the only things you'll need to make the rest of your career a smashing success:

Have pests jump through hoops

The customer will take to his heels

Your colleagues will love you for your efforts

You'll win Employee of the Year

You will be idolized and receive free massages

You can retire to Florida

**Good luck!**

www.ingramcontent.com/pod-product-compliance
Lightning Source LLC
Chambersburg PA
CBHW071303170526
45165CB00003B/1392